THE EASY GARDEN

 MICHAEL GRIFFITHS

THE EASY GARDEN

Month-by-month advice to improve your outside space

CONTENTS

6 INTRODUCTION
10 GETTING STARTED

22 SPRING
76 SUMMER
122 AUTUMN
170 WINTER

216 RESOURCES
217 INDEX
222 ACKNOWLEDGEMENTS
224 ABOUT THE AUTHOR

INTRODUCTION

Gardening shouldn't feel like an overwhelming task, yet for so many people, it does. You stand in a garden centre, staring at rows of plants, bags of compost, and a million different tools, wondering what you actually need and whether you're about to make a very expensive mistake. You plant something, only to watch it wither a few weeks later. You turn to Google for help, but end up lost in a sea of overly technical or conflicting advice.

Sound familiar? That's exactly why I wanted to write this book — the one I needed when I started gardening. My straight-talking guide will help you understand what you actually need to do in your outdoor space to keep it looking its best. Month by month, I will walk you through seasonal tasks, common problems, and practical projects and techniques, so you can dip in and out through the year. You'll find instructional, step-by-step photographs and advice that is free from unnecessary fluff or jargon, hopefully helping you to feel confident in tackling garden jobs. Overall, I hope *The Easy Garden* makes your space feel more manageable and a pleasure to be in.

GETTING STARTED

Getting started in the garden can feel like stepping into a whole new world. You might feel a mix of excitement, curiosity, and maybe a touch of confusion about where to begin. Don't worry, everyone starts there. The truth is, you don't need fancy gear or years of experience to grow something great; you just need a few basics and a bit of know-how. This section will help you find your footing, getting comfortable with the tools of the trade, understanding what makes your garden tick, and building the small habits that make a big difference over time. So, roll up your sleeves, keep an open mind, and enjoy the process. Before long, you'll be wondering how you ever managed without the joy of a good dig, and the satisfaction of watching things grow.

12 What are the essential garden tools?
14 How to prune with secateurs
16 How to test your soil
18 How to pot on perfectly every time
20 How to water plants

What are the essential garden tools?

If I had no tools and had to start all over again, what would my essential garden tools be? When starting out, it's useful to have the right kit. To be frank, it's very annoying when you want to do a job, but you don't have the right tools. So, these are my recommendations.

SECATEURS

If there's one tool every gardener should keep handy, it's a trusty pair of secateurs. Snipping deadheads, trimming unruly stems, or giving roses a much-needed chop. Without them, you'll find yourself wrestling with plants, using kitchen scissors (not recommended), or worse, snapping stems by hand. A good pair makes you feel neat, in control, and just a little bit professional, even if the rest of the garden is still a jungle!

HAND TROWEL

Whether you're in a tight space creating holes, digging out weeds, or scooping compost into pots, a hand trowel always earns its keep. Forget one on the other side of the garden and you'll realize just how often you reach for it. Before you know it, your trowel will quickly become an extension of your hand.

HAND FORK

Perfect for loosening compacted soil, teasing out stubborn weeds, or mixing in compost around plants, a hand fork saves you from doing battle with the ground using just your fingers. Think of it as the trowel's sidekick – less about scooping, more about prodding, prising, and generally making the soil more welcoming for your plants.

BORDER SPADE

A compact version of the classic spade. Smaller, lighter, and much easier to handle than its hefty digging sibling. It's perfect for working in tighter spots and slips neatly into flowerbeds, letting you dig planting holes, edge borders, and divide plants without trampling everything around them.

GETTING STARTED

HORI HORI KNIFE
A hori hori knife is one of those tools that proves its worth in any garden. Part-digging tool, part-weeding knife, it's perfect for planting bulbs, trimming roots, or tackling stubborn weeds. Its sharp, sturdy blade and versatile design mean fewer trips going back and forth for different tools. By adding one to your toolkit, you'll gain a true multitasker.

TWINE
Twine is a humble item that quietly earns its place in every gardener's pocket. Need to tie up a floppy stem, train a climber, or mark out a straight row? Twine's got your back. It's endlessly useful, wonderfully simple, and always runs out just when you need it most. Like duct tape, it's not glamorous but it is indispensable.

HOSE
A hosepipe is the garden's lifeline. It keeps everything from wilting in summer and saves you countless trips with a watering can. It's also a bit of a multitasker: one minute you're giving borders and pots a good soak, the next you're blasting mud off your boots or giving the dog a rinse (if they'll let you!). Once you've got a decent hose, you'll wonder how you managed without one.

WHERE'S THE REST?
Wait... that's it? Well, yes. To me, anything else is situational. If you have a lawn, you'll want a lawn mower. For a hedge, you'll want a hedge trimmer. Don't like getting soil under your nails? You'll need some gloves. My advice is to fill out the rest of your list based on the jobs you have to do.

WHAT YOU NEED

- Secateurs

TECHNIQUE
How to prune with secateurs

Let's get one of the basics down straight away. You might think pruning is a simple case of cutting wherever you like. Depending on the plant, incorrect pruning can lead to a weakened structure, increased susceptibility to disease, pests, and even death. However, if you follow these three simple tips, you'll get it right every time.

Cut at a 45-degree angle, slanting away from the bud

GET THE ANGLE RIGHT
Make cuts at a 45-degree angle for plants with single buds, like roses. This helps prevent water pooling on the cut and promotes healthier growth. Stems on plants with double buds like lavender and hydrangea can be cut across at a 90-degree angle.

WHAT TO REMOVE
Dead, diseased, and damaged branches can be brittle, discoloured, or cracked. When pruning, remove them back to healthy wood with sharp, clean secateurs or loppers to improve airflow, reduce disease, and keep plants healthy and tidy.

Cut back dead wood to where it is green

GETTING STARTED

Cut a short distance above a bud

Prune here to direct growth upwards

THE DISTANCE FROM THE BUD
Cut about 5mm (¼in) above the bud. This distance ensures you're not pruning too close or too far away from the bud.

POWERED VS MANUAL
Powered secateurs save time and effort, making pruning thicker stems easier and reducing hand strain. They are great if you do a lot of gardening or struggle with your hands. Manual secateurs offer more control for lighter, precise cuts and quick jobs.

PRUNE TO DIRECT GROWTH
When pruning a stem, the bud nearest the top of the cut will be the first to produce a new shoot. So, prune just above a bud that points in the direction that you want the new shoot to grow. This is particularly useful for creating the shape of the plant that you want.

WHAT YOU NEED

- A trowel
- A clear jar with straight sides and a lid (Mason jars are perfect)
- 1 tsp washing-up liquid
- A tape measure

TECHNIQUE
How to test your soil

Figuring out what kind of soil you have is a bit like checking the weather before heading out. It lets you know what you're dealing with before diving in. Some soils drink up water and hold on tight, like clay; while others, like sandy soil, let water slip straight through. Then there's loam, which is the happy medium, not too heavy, not too light. Understanding your soil makes picking plants and caring for them a whole lot easier. So how do you work out what kind of soil you have? Here's a simple experiment you can try at home.

1

Dig down about 20cm (8in) and scoop enough soil to fill your jar about halfway.

2

Top it up with water until it's roughly three-quarters full, then add the washing-up liquid and pop the lid on.

GETTING STARTED

Clay
Silt
Sand

4
Measure the height of each layer once the water clears and work out the percentages. Let's say your jar has a total soil depth of 7cm (2¾in): 4.5cm (1¾in) sand, 1.5cm (⅝in) silt, and 1cm (⅜in) clay. That works out to:
- **Sand** 64 per cent
- **Silt** 21 per cent
- **Clay** 15 per cent

3
Shake the jar vigorously for three minutes, put it somewhere and leave it alone. Let it sit for 48 hours. After a while, your soil will start to settle, separating into distinct layers:
- **Sand** is the fastest and heaviest, sinking to the bottom. You might notice a coarse layer and a finer layer above it.
- **Silt** takes a little longer and forms a mid-layer.
- **Clay** is slowest and densest, forming a layer on top of the silt.
- **Bits of floating organic matter?** Leave those, they're not part of the soil calculation.

5
Use a soil texture triangle (**below**) to find out what type of soil that combination represents. Once you have the percentages for each soil type you can follow the lines to where they intersect. In this example the soil is sandy loam.

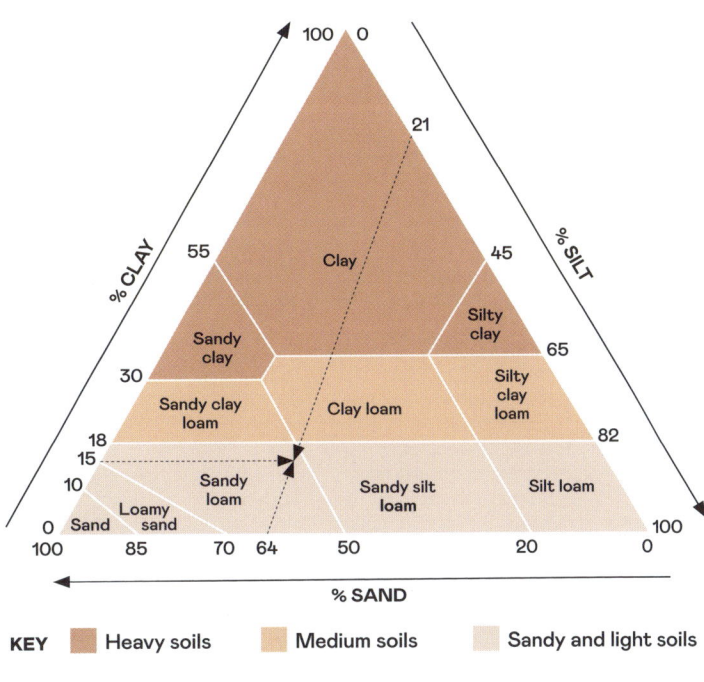

KEY: Heavy soils | Medium soils | Sandy and light soils

17

WHAT YOU NEED

- Pot
- Compost
- Trowel

TECHNIQUE
How to pot on perfectly every time

The easiest way to pot on a plant is to plant it while it's still in a pot. This is one of those tricks that has been around for ages, but it really does make this somewhat tedious job much simpler. It's the same approach whether you're moving a plant to a bigger pot, or planting in the ground, but I'm using a pot in this example.

1
Put some compost in the bottom of the new pot with your trowel, making sure the base is level. Before you go too much further, it's worth making sure that your plant will come free. Sometimes you need to tap the side of the pot or squeeze it.

2
Take your plant and, keeping it in its existing pot, place it in the new pot. Make sure that the top of the soil level on the plant is around 2.5–5cm (1–2in) below the rim of the new pot. This way you'll be able to water it without water spilling over the top.

Make sure the pot is centred. Take a step back and check you're happy with how it looks

GETTING STARTED

4
Lift the plant out again, remove the old pot, and slide it into its perfectly shaped hole.

3
Backfill around the pot with your soil, pushing it down the sides of the pot as you go. Really push it down the sides, so that there are no air pockets.

WHAT YOU NEED

- Hose
- Watering can

TECHNIQUE
How to water plants

You may think it's just a case of pointing a hose or watering can over the top of your plant and you're done. But, if you want to be efficient with your water and minimize the risk of disease, you should follow these tips.

WHAT TO DO
Always aim to water at the base of the plant to prevent waste by directing your watering where it is most needed. This helps prevent fungal diseases, which need moisture on the leaves to germinate, and conserves water by minimizing evaporation from the leaves and flowers.

HOSE SETTINGS

If you have a hose, there are a number of settings that the manufacturers often don't explain, so let me fill in the gaps for you. They may be called alternative names by different brands, but their uses are as follows:

CONE
Best for delicate watering

FINE ROSE
Perfect for general watering

JET
Use for cleaning surfaces

FLAT
Ideal for washing pests off plants

FAST FILL
For filling buckets and watering cans

FINE
Creates a light mist that works well for seedlings

WATERING MYTHS

MYTH 1
WATERING IN FULL SUN WILL BURN YOUR PLANT'S LEAVES

The idea is that the water that falls on your leaves will stay there, creating mini magnifying glasses and burning your plants' leaves. But think about it, when it rains and then sun shines, leaves don't get scorched. The intensity of the sun doesn't matter either, the water on the leaves is just more likely to evaporate faster. If plant leaves appear burnt, it could be due to inadequate watering or nutrient deficiencies, rather than water droplets on leaves.

MYTH 2
YOU SHOULD ONLY WATER IN THE EARLY MORNING OR LATER

This is about water efficiency. For your wallet, and also for your plants, ideally you should water when the plant can take in as much water as possible. That is during the morning or in the evening, but that doesn't mean that these are the only times that you can water. So, if your plant is looking thirsty in the midday sun, you can water it. Yes, you will lose more water due to evaporation and transpiration, but you won't damage the plant by doing this.

MYTH 3
A FINE MIST WILL COOL YOUR PLANTS DOWN

Unless you're working in a controlled greenhouse with a misting system, misting plants is pretty much useless as the water will evaporate.

SPRING

At this time of year your garden is starting to come alive. After the quiet of winter, the soil warms, buds fatten, and bulbs push through with bursts of colour. The weather might remain unpredictable — one minute it's sunny, the next it's hailing — but for the most part, it's a time to start getting back outside. There'll be plenty of new growth, which can swiftly turn into chaos, so keep things simple, pace yourself, and enjoy the show.

MARCH

- **24** How to tidy daffodils and other bulbs
- **25** How to fertilize roses
- **26** How to rejuvenate honeysuckle
- **28** How to prune hydrangeas
- **30** How to remove weeds before they take hold
- **32** How to make your own weedkiller for paths and patios
- **34** How to plant bare-root strawberries
- **36** How to move plants
- **38** How to divide perennials
- **39** How to deal with aphids

APRIL

- **40** How to mow your lawn effectively
- **42** How to use a trimmer like a pro
- **44** How to scarify your lawn
- **46** How to aerate your lawn
- **48** How to overseed your lawn
- **50** How to grow a clover lawn
- **52** How to start dahlia tubers
- **54** How to create a border in the shade
- **56** How to protect your plants from slugs and snails
- **58** How to pressure wash your patio

MAY

- **60** How to harden off plants
- **61** How to spring prune lavender
- **62** How to prune ornamental olive trees
- **64** How to prune an evergreen hedge
- **66** How to propagate plants in water
- **68** How to deadhead roses for more blooms
- **69** How to treat roses with black spot
- **70** How to tie in climbing plants
- **72** How to create a hanging basket
- **74** How to do the Chelsea chop

WHAT YOU NEED

- Secateurs
- Bamboo cane (optional)
- Plant feed

TECHNIQUE
How to tidy daffodils and other bulbs

Daffodils, tulips, and their cousins are some of the easiest plants you can grow. Bulbs are tough, low-maintenance, and most will happily pop up year after year with barely a thought from you. That said, a little TLC goes a long way if you want them looking their absolute best.

WHY DO THIS NOW
You can tidy your bulbs as soon as they have finished flowering. For some varieties, such as daffodils, that will be now, while others, such as alliums, may not bloom until later in the year. You can follow the same steps for all your bulbs.

1
After your bulbs have flowered, get rid of the spent heads. If you have tiny clumps snip them off by hand, taking off the head and leaving the stalk. If you have larger bunches, grab a slender cane (like a bamboo cane) and use it to whip the heads off above the leaves — quick, satisfying, and a little bit fun.

2
Feed them while the leaves are still green. Use a feed that is high in **potassium** (tomato fertilizer works brilliantly) and keep feeding every 7–10 days until the foliage yellows.

LEAVE THE LEAVES
Don't cut or tie up the green leaves; they're busy storing energy into the bulb to make next year's flowers. Only remove the foliage when it has gone yellow and floppy.

MARCH

WHAT YOU NEED

- Hand fork
- Plant feed
- Watering can

TECHNIQUE
How to fertilize roses

If you want loads of flowers on your roses this year, now is the perfect time to feed them. There are plenty of feeds out there, but I like to go with a controlled-release feed, which, with one application, will nourish your rose all summer long.

WHY DO THIS NOW
Feeding roses in early spring as they begin to grow but before they flower will ensure they have the goodness they need to grow strong shoots and put on a great show of flowers.

1
Clear any weeds and debris from around your roses. I like to use a hand fork for this job.

2
Measure out the food to make sure you're giving your plants the right amount. A lot of controlled-release feeds come in pellet form with a cup, so you don't need to guess. Pour the feed around the base of your roses and then lightly agitate the soil using your fork. Try to get it in the soil, not just sitting on the top, to minimize the risk of it being blown or washed away by wind or rain.

3
Water the plant if you're not expecting rain soon. Now your roses are fed and ready to give you bigger and better blooms.

WHAT YOU NEED

- Secateurs
- Tape measure

TECHNIQUE
How to rejuvenate honeysuckle

You know it's time for some drastic action if your plant looks whippy and unruly. I'm particularly guilty of this. I love honeysuckle in the summer, but I let it go wild because I love the look. Sadly, it is then an absolute mess the following year, so I always cut it back in early spring to recover it.

WHY DO THIS NOW
This is the time when honeysuckle is about to put on spring growth so cutting back now will stimulate plenty of new shoots and help you keep its shape neat.

1
Cut the whole plant down to around 60cm (2ft), and the plant will respond with a lot of new shoots. No need to be delicate or cut above a bud – just take it all right down.

MARCH

A LIGHTER TOUCH
If your honeysuckle doesn't need such drastic action, give it a light tidy-up once the blooms fade by snipping out any dead, damaged, or weedy stems and trimming back any overgrown bits to keep a nice shape.

2
Strengthen the plant by removing weak, damaged, or dead stems. If there are any crossed branches, remove or untangle them.

3
You should now be left with your strongest and best-placed stems. This might look aggressive but, trust me, it's going to be fine.

WHAT YOU NEED

- Tape measure
- Secateurs

TECHNIQUE
How to prune hydrangeas

People have varying ideas about when hydrangeas should be pruned and there are different rules depending on the type you have. There are two types of hydrangea — those that flower on new wood and those that flower on old wood. It's important to know which you have, as each is pruned differently.

WHY DO THIS NOW
Prune hydrangeas in spring, after the risk of frost has passed, to promote strong new growth. Keep an eye on the weather rather than the date. While you can also safely prune softwood hydrangeas in autumn, pruning now is the safest bet to guarantee flowers on all varieties.

PRUNING NEW WOOD

Hydrangeas that flower on new wood, such as panicle hydrangeas or smooth-barked varieties like "Annabelle" (**below**), can be pruned a lot harder than those that flower on old wood.

1
Prune at a 90-degree angle to a height of around 30cm (12in) just above a pair of healthy buds on each stem and repeat over the whole plant. This may take a while if you have a few plants, but they will look much better for it later in the year.

MARCH

PRUNING OLD WOOD

To prune hydrangeas that flower on old wood, for example bigleaf varieties such as *Hydrangea macrophylla* or oakleaf hydrangea like *Hydrangea quercifolia* (**below**), follow the steps below.

1
Remove old flower heads at a 90-degree angle to just above a pair of buds. Hydrangea buds can easily be knocked off, so cut carefully with your secateurs.

2
Cut out thin, weak stems (less than the width of a pencil), as well as removing any crossing, dead, or hollow stems.

3
If your plant is looking congested, remove one or two of the largest, oldest stems from as low down as possible to promote new shoots from the base. The oldest stems will be thick and woody at the base, and may even have peeling bark.

WHAT YOU NEED

- Garden fork, hoe, trowel, or hori hori knife
- Kettle or weed burner
- Spinning wire brush or weed puller

TROUBLESHOOTING
How to remove weeds before they take hold

Weeds are cheeky things. The minute spring even thinks about starting, they're already up and running, often weeks before our carefully planted flowers get going. There isn't a single "one-size-fits-all" way to deal with weeds — what works in a border won't always work on the patio — but here are some tried-and-tested methods that I keep coming back to.

WHY DO THIS NOW
If you don't stay on top of the weeds early in the year, they'll spread, set seed, and turn into a much bigger headache later in the season.

AVOID CHEMICAL WEEDKILLERS
While these work quickly and can keep weeds away for longer, they come with serious downsides: damage to soil life, runoff into the environment, and potential harm to pets and kids. If I need something extra, I make up my own weedkiller (see pp.32–33) rather than reaching for a shop-bought spray.

HAND TOOLS
Sometimes, the old-fashioned way really is the best. Grab a garden fork, hoe, trowel, or a hori hori knife (**right**) and dig out the weeds. Sometimes you can pull them out by hand (**left**). The key is to get the roots, especially with weeds like bindweed or nettles, where even the tiniest bit left in the soil can bounce back into a whole new plant.

Pro tip: weeding after rain is much easier because the soil loosens up and roots slide out cleanly.

MARCH

BOILING WATER (OR HEAT)

Pouring boiling water onto small weeds in cracks and paving (**left**) can kill off weeds by bursting their cells. It's cheap and chemical-free, but you'll need a few goes for anything with deeper roots, and you need to be careful around your toes, pets, and nearby plants. If you like the heat approach, a weed burner (**right**) is a lot easier (and safer) than constantly running back and forth with the kettle.

MECHANICAL REMOVAL

There are some clever tools out there designed to make weeding less of a back-breaker. For patios and driveways, spinning wire-brush cleaners (**right**) are brilliant. On lawns, a weed puller (**left**) can pop dandelions out like magic, though they're a bit chunky for borders. It really comes down to matching the right tool to the right job, but when you do, it can save a lot of time and sore knees.

WHAT YOU NEED

- Large jug
- 1 litre (4 cups) white or acetic vinegar
- 3 tbsp table salt
- 1 tbsp washing-up liquid
- Spray bottle

PROJECT
How to make your own weedkiller for paths and patios

If you're keen to ditch weeds without resorting to harsh chemicals, this DIY mix is a handy option. It uses everyday ingredients you probably already have in the kitchen: vinegar, salt, and a bit of washing-up liquid. The vinegar and salt work together to dry weeds out, while the soap helps the mix stick to the leaves by cutting through their natural waxy coating.

WHY DO THIS NOW
It's good to tackle the weeds before they have the chance to become established later in the year and become more difficult to deal with.

HOW TO MAKE IT

Pour the vinegar into the jug, add the salt, then the washing-up liquid (in that order). Swirl it around but don't shake it. Pour it into your spray bottle and use as needed, then refill.

MARCH

HOW TO USE IT

Pick a sunny, dry day. Spray directly onto the weeds until the leaves are wet but not dripping. Sunlight really helps this mix to be effective, so avoid using it if rain's due later because it will just wash away before it gets a chance to work. You should see the weeds starting to curl and brown within about eight hours.

AVOID BEDS, BORDERS, AND POTS
Apply weedkiller to paths and patios but avoid spraying it onto raised beds or anywhere else you're growing food. Just be aware that it can stop anything from growing in that spot for a long while.

WHAT YOU NEED

- Bare-root strawberry plants
- Jug or watering can
- Compost

TECHNIQUE
How to plant bare-root strawberries

Runners are bare-root strawberry plants that are available in the winter. They're a wonderful fruiting plant you can easily grow in your garden as they don't take up much space. Some varieties can even be grown in hanging baskets. If you're growing them in a bed, choose an area with sun for at least half the day and make sure it's raked level before you begin.

WHY DO THIS NOW

Early spring after the last frost is the ideal time to plant bare-root strawberries. If you miss that window, the next best time is early autumn. Only do this after the threat of frost has passed. As this differs depending on where you are, check your local weather.

1
Soak your runners as soon as they arrive in tepid water for an hour before planting.

2
Unwrap them and identify the crown, this is the bit in the middle above the roots but below the leaves.

MARCH

3
Add compost to your pot or flowerbed, then dig a hole large enough to spread the roots in, make a mound in the middle, and place the crown on the mound. Gently spread the roots around the plant and make sure the crown sits on the surface of the soil so it doesn't either rot or dry out. Firm the soil around the roots with your hands.

4
Repeat this process every 30cm (12in) if you're growing multiple plants. Check the soil every other day for the first two weeks. It needs to be kept moist. If you're not sure, push your finger 5–10cm (2–4in) into the soil around the roots to check.

WHEN THEY ARRIVE
If you're not able to plant your strawberry runners immediately, they can be kept in the fridge for a few days, as long as you keep the roots moist.

WHAT YOU NEED

- Watering can
- Spade
- Hori hori knife

TECHNIQUE
How to move plants

You might want to move a plant because it's got too big for a particular location, it's not flourishing where it is, or you may be redesigning your garden. It can be difficult to know how and when to move plants without causing them stress and damage. The process is the same regardless of what kind of plant you're moving.

WHY DO THIS NOW

Spring is a great time to shift plants around because the soil is warming up, there is usually enough rain to keep things moist, and plants are only just waking up, so they handle the move better. Once replanted, they've got the whole growing season to settle their roots in before winter. Just avoid frosty spells or blazing hot weather when they'll struggle to cope.

1

Before you move the plant, give it a good soak — this will help support it when it's moved. Even better, water the soil well the day before and remove any nearby weeds so you don't take them with you.

2

Dig the new hole before moving the plant to minimize the amount of time it spends out of the ground. At the same time you can make sure there's room to reposition the plant and deal with any surprises, such as tree roots or compacted soil, at the new site.

MARCH

3

Start digging out your plant using a spade. The more root you can take and the less damage you do to it, the easier it is for the plant to re-establish. Avoid pulling plants out by the stem because it may rip off. You may need to use a garden knife, or similar, to cut some roots if you can't dig a deep enough hole.

4

Gently place the plant in the new hole. Backfill soil into the hole around the plant until its soil is level with the surrounding ground.

5

Finally, water in and top dress with 5cm (2in) of mulch (see pp.168–169) to retain moisture. Firm in gently with your hands.

WHAT YOU NEED

- Spade or fork
- Hori hori knife

TECHNIQUE
How to divide perennials

Dividing your own plants is relatively quick and easy to do and will provide you with plants you already love for free. Many perennials can be divided. Anything that forms a clump with multiple stems is ideal. If you dig it up and see a big, fibrous, rooty mass it's normally ok to divide. If the plant grows from a deep tap root or has a woody base, it's better to take cuttings or grow a new plant from seed instead.

WHY DO THIS NOW
Spring is the perfect time for dividing perennials because they're just waking up and the soil is warm and moist. Splitting them now also gives plants a whole season to settle, grow strong, and flower later.

1
Grab a spade or fork and dig around the plant, making sure you take as many of the roots with you as possible. Gently lift the whole thing out of the ground. If your plant is in a pot, give the pot a tap to loosen the plant and then take it out.

2
Shake off some soil so you can see the roots but don't forget to look at the top. Some plants will split easily into clumps so you can see where to cut them.

3
Split the plant — some can be teased apart with your fingers while others need a bit more force with a knife or spade. Just make sure each chunk has a few shoots and enough roots to anchor the plant.

4
Watch for sap coming from the cut, known as bleeding. A small amount is fine, but if your plant is bleeding a lot, place it in a shaded spot and wait 24 hours for it to dry before planting to avoid rot.

5
Replant each section at the same depth it was before and firm in. Give each one space and water regularly.

MARCH

WHAT YOU NEED

- Hosepipe
- 5 tbsp washing-up liquid
- 1 litre (4 cups) water
- Spray bottle

TROUBLESHOOTING
How to deal with aphids

Aphids, also known as greenfly or blackfly, are tiny, sap-sucking bugs that love soft, new plant growth. They come in many colours from green and black to yellow, brown, and orange and are mostly a spring and summer problem. The good news is that most types only target specific plants, so an infestation on one plant doesn't automatically mean your whole garden is doomed.

WHY DO THIS NOW
Early in the season, aphid numbers might rise sharply before predators have a chance to catch up. If you're concerned, you can tackle them now with the steps below. If you can wait, ladybirds, lacewings, hoverflies, damsel bugs, and parasitic wasps all eat aphids. Leaving these garden helpers alone or even encouraging them with planting can keep aphids in check naturally.

1
Check your plants regularly, as early detection is key. Aphids hide in leaf joints and under leaves. Sticky honeydew sap or ants marching up stems can be your first clue that they are present.

2
Blast the aphids with water, hand-pick or gently brush them off the plant if you only have a minor infestation.

3
Make your own soap and water spray for larger infestations by mixing washing-up liquid and water in a spray bottle. Shake it and spray the mixture directly onto the infested leaves and stems, covering the aphids. Repeat weekly until things calm down.

WHAT YOU NEED

- Lawnmower

TECHNIQUE
How to mow your lawn effectively

Mowing the lawn is a straightforward task but there are a few additional tips that will make your life easier, and your grass look better.

WHY DO THIS NOW

Start mowing your lawn now and continue to do it whenever it gets long. In spring and early summer, you'll probably be mowing about once a week, but if growth slows or the weather is dry, every couple of weeks is fine. In autumn, once every week or two should do. Just don't hack off more than a third of the grass at a time and it will be happy and healthy.

THE BEST TIME TO MOW YOUR LAWN

The best time to mow your lawn is when the grass is dry and not baking in the sun. Late morning or early evening are the best times as the dew has dried but the sun isn't at its highest.

APRIL

COMMON PROBLEMS

THE LAWNMOWER IS CLOGGING
In the early morning, there will likely still be dew on the grass. While there is nothing unsafe about mowing wet grass, your lawnmower will have to work harder and clumps of wet grass may clog it and accumulate in your garden. If you have to mow a wet lawn, you can mitigate this by doing a pass on your highest mower setting first, then moving down.

SOIL COMPACTION AND SLOW GROWTH
To encourage stronger growth and avoid soil compaction, mix up your mowing patterns with each cut for a healthier lawn. This way you won't make ruts in your lawn, and you'll catch the blades of grass that may have bent out of the way the last time. Cut in straight lines horizontally, vertically, and diagonally so your lawn doesn't compact in the same areas.

PATCHY GRASS
As tempting as it may be, taking too much off at once will stress out your grass. The proper height for your grass will depend on its species. But one thing everyone agrees on is that you should never remove more than one-third of your grass on any single cutting. So adjust the height on your mower and cut your grass down in increments. This will reduce the amount of stress you put on the grass.

WHAT YOU NEED

- Trimmer
- Bucket
- Goggles

TECHNIQUE
How to use a trimmer like a pro

A grass trimmer is a great tool if your grass or part of your garden is very overgrown or you have areas that you can't reach with the lawnmower. While the tool is quite straightforward to use, there are a few extra tips that can be useful at this time of year, especially if your trimmer has been locked up all winter.

WHY DO THIS NOW
This can be done at any time during the spring or summer when you need to trim your grass or undergrowth, although April is the time when the weather is warming up and the grass is beginning to grow after the winter.

1
Soak your trimming line in water before use to extend its life and keep it flexible. If you've stored it for a while, remove the line and soak it in a bucket of water for 24 hours before first use.

2
Check the spin direction of your trimmer. Not all grass trimmers go in the same direction. If yours spins anticlockwise, it will throw out cut grass from the left side, making the right side more effective for trimming and vice versa. No hack required here, just turn it on and see what it does.

APRIL

3
Put on your goggles and trim the growth in stages, whether you're cutting grass or overgrown areas, gradually lowering the trimmer with each pass rather than cutting it all at once. The lower parts are denser and can cause clogging so working in stages helps to keep things moving. Strimming in stages also gives creatures a chance to evacuate.

4
Get a super neat edge to your lawn using your trimmer, moving slowly and letting the cutting line do the work for you.

- **LOOK OUT FOR OBSTACLES**
- If you're using a trimmer to cut back areas
- of undergrowth that have become extremely
- overgrown, work from the outside in, moving
- the trimmer in wide arcs. Look out for
- hidden obstacles like rocks or tree stumps
- and wear goggles to protect your eyes.

WHAT YOU NEED

- Lawnmower
- Spring-tine rake
- Scarifier (optional)
- Moss killer
- Grass seed
- Top-dressing

TECHNIQUE
How to scarify your lawn

If your lawn is starting to look tired, patchy, or just a bit sad, it could be smothered under a layer of thatch and moss. Scarifying is like giving it a deep clean, it clears out the debris, lets the grass breathe, and makes way for healthy new growth. In a few weeks, you'll see thicker, healthier grass that's far better equipped to thrive. There are two ways to do it, depending on your lawn size and energy levels.

WHY DO THIS NOW
As the grass is growing at this time of year it can recover from the process before the heat of the summer. For the same reason, this could also be done in early autumn.

MANUAL SCARIFICATION

For a quick tidy-up over a smaller area use a tine rake to scarify your lawn.

1
Mow the lawn short (see pp.40–41) to make the job easier before you start scarifying.

2
Take a flexible spring-tine rake, and gently but firmly pull it back through the grass multiple times, working in a criss-cross pattern over the whole lawn. This helps lift out dead grass, moss, and built-up thatch.

APRIL

HOW TO TREAT MOSS IN YOUR LAWN

Treat the area with a moss killer to blacken what's left after scarifying. Once it's dead (usually after a week or so, depending on what you use), give the lawn another light rake to clear away the debris. Sprinkle fresh grass seed over any bare patches and they'll green up again in no time.

Stop the moss from simply coming back by aerating the lawn (see pp.46–47) to improve drainage, then adding a light top-dressing (see p.49). This will improve the soil and help the grass grow stronger, making it harder for moss to muscle its way back in.

MECHANICAL SCARIFICATION

If you have a large lawn you might want to either buy or hire a scarifier to get the job done more quickly.

1
Adjust the scarifier to the correct height so the bladed drum skims through the thatch without cutting too deeply. Aim to remove most of the debris but leave a little thatch to protect the soil from drying out or washing away.

2
Repeat, working at right angles to your first run. Once you've finished, collect all the debris, then follow up by aerating and overseeding your lawn (see pp.46–49).

WHAT YOU NEED

- Fork, hollow-tine aerator, or mechanical aerator
- Horticultural sand

TECHNIQUE
How to aerate your lawn

Relieving soil compaction, supporting drainage, and allowing air, water, and nutrients to penetrate the grass roots where they are needed most — aerating your lawn is a simple job that has huge benefits. This can be done using a garden fork or a mechanical aerator — ideal if you have a larger lawn or want to save your back.

WHY DO THIS NOW
This is best done when your grass is actively growing, so spring or autumn are both suitable. Avoid summer as heat and drought will make the grass vulnerable.

MANUAL AERATION

A quick and effective way to aerate your lawn without using machinery is to use a garden fork. A hollow-tine aerator (**above**) does the same job.

1
Plunge the fork or aerator about 10cm (4in) into the soil. Lean it back slightly to open up the space, and pull it out.

2
Repeat this process every 15cm (6in) across the lawn.

3
Leave the holes open or fill them with horticultural sand to improve the drainage further.

APRIL

MECHANICAL AERATION

An aerator can speed up the job if you have a larger area to cover. It's probably best to hire one so that you don't need to store it for the rest of the year.

1
Push the aerator steadily over the lawn from left to right, covering it evenly.

2
Leave the holes open or fill them with horticultural sand.

TYPES OF SAND
Horticultural sand is coarser than the sand you find on the beach. This helps trap air and increase aeration and drainage. You can also add it to lawns with heavy clay soils to help reduce soil compaction.

WHAT YOU NEED

- Lawnmower
- Hori hori knife
- Fertilizer
- Grass seed
- Seed spreader (optional)
- Top-dressing
- Hosepipe
- Netting (optional)

TECHNIQUE
How to overseed your lawn

After winter your lawn can look a little rough around the edges, so it's a good idea to sow new seeds to repair patches and improve density. It's a good idea to scarify and aerate your lawn first (see pp.44–47). The main types of seed mix are general purpose, fine lawn, shade tolerant, and rapid growth, so choose what works for your situation. You don't need to match the type that's already there as they will work together.

WHY DO THIS NOW

Spring provides the perfect conditions for lawn care as the nights aren't too cold and the days aren't too warm. You can, however, do this job in the autumn.

1

Mow the lawn so that you can see which areas are in need of overseeding. Mowing to a height of around 3cm (1in) will do the trick.

2

Pull up any perennial weeds growing in the grass and fill the holes that are left behind with topsoil or compost. You can use a hori hori knife to cut the weed out from the root, so it doesn't return.

APRIL

3
Moisten the soil and apply a fertilizer before overseeding (check the instructions on your fertilizer). Make sure there is no weed- or moss killer in the fertilizer, as this will prevent the grass seed from germinating. Lawn fertilizers come in granular and liquid feeds. I prefer liquid feeds here as they are faster acting.

PATCH REPAIR
If you have a small patch to repair and don't want to overseed the whole lawn, start by clearing out any obvious weeds and getting rid of dead grass. Ensure the area is clear before laying any seeds. If the ground is compacted you can fork it over first to agitate the soil. Rake the area level, add some compost then shake the seeds evenly over the top. Rake in gently and firm with your feet before watering carefully to avoid disturbing any seeds. I use this process when I've removed a large weed, or my dog has repeatedly peed on one patch of grass.

4
Spread the seed over the areas where it is needed. A light covering is fine — you should still be able to see soil through the seeds. If you have a large area, a seed spreader can be really handy.

5
Cover the seeds lightly with top-dressing (a thin layer of sand, soil, or a mix of the two), which will retain moisture and help to discourage birds. Finally, water your lawn every day until your grass is established. If you really struggle with birds taking seeds you might want to consider netting the area to keep them off.

WHAT YOU NEED

- Lawnmower
- Tine rake or scarifier
- Fork
- Fertilizer (optional)
- Clover seed
- Seed spreader (optional)
- Watering can or hosepipe

PROJECT
How to grow a clover lawn

If you want to add more biodiversity to your lawn but aren't ready to rip it up and sow a wildflower meadow, a clover lawn can be a great step. You can sow a 100 per cent clover lawn or go for a mix of clover and grass. Clover isn't as hard-wearing, so a mix will allow your lawn to withstand foot traffic and won't need regular overseeding, while still providing benefits to your local wildlife.

WHY DO THIS NOW
The best time to do this is spring or autumn when the grass is growing fastest.

1
Mow, scarify, and aerate before sowing. If you want, you could use a fertilizer with phosphorus and potassium to aid establishment but avoid anything with nitrogen. A nitrogen-heavy fertilizer will favour the grass growth over that of the clover.

WHY GROW CLOVER?
A clover lawn is easier to maintain and better for wildlife than plain grass. It stays lush through dry spells, needs less mowing, and naturally crowds out weeds, so you get a softer, low-maintenance lawn. Because clover fixes nitrogen in the soil, it feeds your lawn for free, saving you from buying fertilizer. On top of that, its flowers are a magnet for bees and butterflies.

APRIL

2
Spread the clover seeds over the area you want to seed by hand and cover them with a fine layer of topsoil. Since they're much smaller than grass seeds, you might find it difficult to find a spreader that can hold them.

3
Make sure the seeds are in contact with the soil by walking over the area to press them down. Water every day for two weeks, and you should soon see the beginnings of clover in your lawn.

WHAT YOU NEED

- Dahlia tubers
- Large shallow tray or pot
- Compost
- Hosepipe

TECHNIQUE
How to start dahlia tubers

Dahlias are loved for their diverse shapes, vibrant colour, and long flowering period and are particularly great in flower arrangements. I sometimes feel there is a little trepidation around growing them, but they're relatively easy, especially if you get started early on in the season.

WHY DO THIS NOW
Planting dahlia tubers in April when the soil and air are warming up gives them a longer growing season, so they have plenty of time to grow big and bloom beautifully over summer.

1
Find the top of the tuber. Dahlias are happiest planted on their sides, and positioning the tuber the right way up is important. Look for the old stem sticking up, or a new, pink shoot, which is the new growth — this is the top.

The top of the tuber

APRIL

2
Plant the tubers in a large, shallow tray or individually in a large pot of compost with drainage holes. Lightly cover them with damp compost and tuck them in so they sit just below the soil surface. At this time of year, you're not planting the tubers properly, just encouraging them to grow a bit bigger, so don't plant them too deep, keeping the new growth on top.

3
Water them well, and put them in a light, frost-free place such as a greenhouse, cold frame, or windowsill. New shoots should start to form after about five weeks, and you'll have a bushy plant by the time the frosts have ended that is ready to plant out.

DAHLIA VARIETIES

There are many different forms and colours of dahlias available. Just a few are shown here.

CACTUS

POMPON

COLLARETTE

DECORATIVE

WHAT YOU NEED

- Shady plants according to height
- Spade
- Trowel
- Compost

PROJECT
How to create a border in the shade

Don't write off that dark corner of your garden. Shady spots can be turned into lush, leafy retreats with the right plants. The trick is to focus on texture, foliage colour, and seasonal flowers that thrive in dappled light or even full shade.

WHY DO THIS NOW
At this time of year the soil is warmer and damper, which is easier for digging up and planting new arrangements. Planting now will also give you the full growing season ahead for your new border to flourish.

TYPES OF SHADE
First, decide what kind of shade you have:

- **Partial shade** Three to six hours per day of direct sun at midsummer.
- **Moderate shade** Two or three hours of direct sun each day at midsummer.
- **Full shade** Less than two hours of direct sun per day in midsummer.

Knowing this will help you pick plants that will thrive in those conditions. Most of those shown opposite do well in partial to full shade.

PLAN YOUR LAYERS
A shady border works best if you think in layers. That way, you've always got a mix of heights, textures, and colours.

- **Tall and dramatic at the back** — think ferns or hostas with big leaves.
- **Mid-height fillers in the middle** — try astilbes and heucheras.
- **Low growers and groundcover at the front** — look for pulmonarias and brunneras.

SHADY BORDER PLANTING PLAN
This plan for a 3 x 1.5m (10 x 5ft) border with partial to moderate shade shows how you can position plants of varying heights to get a balanced look.

KEY

- Ferns
- Hostas
- Pulmonarias
- Astilbes
- Heucheras
- Shade grasses
- Brunneras

APRIL

RECOMMENDATIONS FOR A GORGEOUS SHADY BORDER

PULMONARIA
Bee magnets in the spring, pulmonarias thrive in partial to full shade and have speckled leaves and clusters of flowers. They're also low-growing and great for the front of borders.

BRUNNERA
Extremely hardy, brunneras bring clouds of bright blue flowers in spring. Slugs and snails don't bother them much, which is perfect for a partially or fully shaded, damp spot.

HEUCHERA
Available in practically every shade — deep red, lime-green, smoky purple, even silvery tones. Heucheras pop up with dainty flowers in summer and are lovely in the middle of a border or in pots in partial shade.

ASTILBE
This beauty has big, ferny leaves topped with frothy, feathery flower plumes from late spring through summer. Astilbes are great if you want to add height and softness in the middle of a partially shaded border.

HOSTA
Lovers of partial or full shade, hostas' leaves come in endless shapes and colours — striped, spotted, tiny, or dinner-plate sized. Pair them with ferns for a lush, woodland look at the back of a border. They are slug and snail magnets, so be vigilant.

FERNS
Add instant woodland charm to partial or fully shaded areas with ferns. Mix varieties for different frond shapes and textures. Perfect for filling gaps and softening the edges and back of a shady border.

WHAT YOU NEED

- Torch
- Gloves
- Bucket
- Sand, grit, wool pellets, sawdust, or coffee grounds
- Nematodes
- Container
- Beer
- Copper rings

TROUBLESHOOTING
How to protect your plants from slugs and snails

Slugs and snails are one of those pests that every gardener has to deal with. They love nothing more than nibbling ragged holes in leaves and stems, demolishing seedlings overnight, and leaving that telltale slime trail behind. The truth is, you'll never have a completely slug-free garden — so the trick is to protect the plants they love most (like hostas, dahlias, delphiniums, and young seedlings) and use a mix of tactics to keep numbers down.

WHY DO THIS NOW
Slugs and snails are around most of the year, but spring is when they're at their most destructive, feasting on tender new growth.

WOOL
Creating a barrier with wool can stop snails and slugs reaching your plants.

BUILD A BALANCED GARDEN
Birds, frogs, toads, newts, hedgehogs, and slow worms will all eat slugs. So think about ways to invite them in. Adding a pond, log pile, compost heap, hedge, or shrubbery for shelter, or leaving a small gap in your fence so that hedgehogs can wander through, creates habitats that encourage predators to do the work for you. Healthy soil also means stronger plants that are better at shrugging off slug damage, so mulch with compost or manure to keep your beds in good shape.

REMOVE THEM BY HAND
It's not glamorous, but heading out with a torch after dark is still one of the most effective methods to remove slugs and snails. They're busiest about two hours after dusk, so that's your window. Wear gloves if you like, collect them into a bucket, and dispose of them however you see fit. You can make the job easier by baiting them first — leave out old veg leaves, cat biscuits, or bran in one spot, then scoop them up when they gather. During the day, check under pots, boards, stones, and damp corners for slugs and their eggs (clusters of tiny, pearl-like balls). Rake over soil in spring to expose eggs to birds and centipedes.

PUT UP BARRIERS
It's said that slugs and snails avoid crossing rough or sharp textures. Things like sand, grit, wool pellets, sawdust, or coffee grounds can act as barriers — but only when they're dry. Once wet, most barriers act like a slug highway so keep them topped up. Although, remember most slugs live under the soil, not just on the surface, so this won't stop them all.

APRIL

NEMATODES
These microscopic worms protect against slugs and snails.

COPPER RINGS
Pop these around plants. They may cause an unpleasant sensation in slugs and snails so they turn back.

METALLIC SOLUTION
Copper rings are another way of deterring slugs and snails. Snail and slug mucus reacts with the copper, creating an electrical charge that repels them from the plants they surround. This is probably only useful for one or two larger plants.

USE NEMATODES
If you prefer a biological option, nematodes are tiny worms that infect and kill slugs underground. You mix them in water and apply to the soil in the evening when it is mild (above 5°C/41°F) and moist. They work for about six weeks, so you'll need to reapply throughout the growing season. This can be an expensive option if you want to cover your whole garden but works well for targeted areas and raised beds.

SET BEER TRAPS
This traditional method of dealing with slugs and snails isn't to everyone's liking but has been used for a long time and is effective. Get a dedicated trap or sink a container into the ground so the rim is just above soil level, half-fill with beer, and cover it loosely so snails and slugs can still get in but other creatures won't fall in. Slugs are drawn to the smell and drown in the trap. It's best to place these traps on the edges of borders, rather than right in the middle, otherwise they'll snack on your plants on the way.

PLANT WISELY
Sometimes it's easier to work with nature than against it. If one particular plant keeps getting munched, consider swapping it for a more slug-resistant alternative. Slugs usually leave tough, glossy, hairy, or strongly scented leaves alone, so adding more of these into your planting scheme can save you frustration.

BEER TRAP
Setting a beer trap is an effective method of killing slugs and snails.

WHAT YOU NEED

- Pressure washer

TECHNIQUE
How to pressure wash your patio

Don't damage your patio while pressure washing this year. With a high-power jet wash it's easy to lose your jointing material or chip and crack the edges of the slabs. Follow these steps to make sure that doesn't happen.

WHY DO THIS NOW
Spring is a great time to do this so that your outside space is ready for summer.

1
Adjust the pressure washer to find a suitable setting for the job you're doing — you won't necessarily need the highest setting. You can test it on a small area first to make sure it's correct and won't damage your patio.

2
Hold the wand 50cm (20in) from the paving and at a 45-degree angle to the surface of the stone and position yourself so that you don't get covered in muck or soaked in water. Try to work diagonally from one corner.

APRIL

3
Work across the patio diagonally to the direction of the slabs so you don't run along the joints. Pass slowly over the slabs in a sweeping pattern to make sure you cover them evenly. There's no need to hammer the same spot, but you can overlap slightly on each pass to make sure you've cleaned everything thoroughly.

CHOOSING A PRESSURE WASHER
People buying new pressure washers can often be swayed by the bar (pressure) number. While pressure output is important, there's another factor which is often hidden – the flow rate. One of around 5–8 litres (1–2 gallons) per minute is good for cleaning garden furniture while 8–10 litres (2 gallons) per minute is best for patios and brickwork. It's also worth also checking that the pressure can be adjusted and that the machine has wheels and a reel to make moving it around easier. An optional extra is to have dedicated detergent buckets.

WHAT YOU NEED

- Cold frame (optional)
- Fleece or cloche

TECHNIQUE
How to harden off plants

By late spring, the risk of frost is usually over, which means it's safe to start moving tender plants outside. But don't rush them straight from a cosy greenhouse into the garden. Chilly nights can still scorch their leaves and strong winds can tear them up. Instead, you need to gradually get them used to life outdoors by putting them out during the day and protecting them at night – a process known as "hardening off".

WHY DO THIS NOW

This is the time when the weather is starting to warm up and you can think about eventually moving tender plants outside. Cold, wet soil will stunt roots, so hold off planting on if the ground hasn't warmed up. Tropical plants often need another month before they're truly safe outside, but even houseplants can enjoy some fresh air in the warmest months. Also keep an eye on local weather as surprise frosts can still happen.

1
Use a cold frame if you have one. Shut the lid at night, open it during the day, and after a fortnight your plants will be much tougher and better prepared for the elements. If you're not using a cold frame, place plants outside once the temperature starts to warm up in the day and bring them back inside before the nighttime chill. While they're outside, place them in a protected area.

2
Always check the weather forecast and either bring plants back in or cover them with a fleece or cloche for protection if a cold night is on the cards.

3
Remember, tender young growth is slug and snail heaven. Take steps to deter them early (see pp.56–57), or your carefully hardened-off plants could become dinner overnight.

TECHNIQUE
How to spring prune lavender

WHAT YOU NEED
- Secateurs

No one wants a lavender that's gone leggy and twiggy. To achieve a lush, compact plant, prune new growth by around a third.

WHY DO THIS NOW
Prune lavender in the spring? Are you mad? Well, no. If you missed pruning your lavender in late summer, or if the new growth is untidy or frost-damaged, then mid- to late spring, when new growth appears, is an ideal time to prune. Pruning in spring will delay flowering slightly, but in the end you're going to get a shrub with a better shape that will flower for longer.

1
Look for new growth. You can tell this by the colour – new season growth will be on a green stem and old growth brown and woody.

2
Prune new growth back by a third, just above where the new growth starts, shaping the lavender into a compact shrub. Avoid cutting brown, old growth as it may not regrow and you could lose the plant.

WHAT YOU NEED

- Secateurs
- Handsaw

TECHNIQUE
How to prune ornamental olive trees

While this approach won't maximize your fruit yield, it is going to keep your ornamental trees looking lush, especially if they're coming out of winter looking a little worse for wear.

WHY DO THIS NOW

Any time between late spring and early summer is a good time to prune your olive tree, after the risk of frost has passed. Take the same approach whether you have a tree in a pot or planted in the ground.

1
Remove growth that is dead or weak using secateurs or a handsaw. Don't worry about cutting too much — olive trees are hardy and don't suffer from dieback. Be thorough. While your tree may look good from the outside, it may be sparse on the interior and need a prune.

2
Cut out any crossing branches that could rub against each other and cause disease.

MAY

3
Take out any shoots around the base (these are known as water shoots). **Left** before. **Right** after.

4
Prune branches above a bud to shape the tree. From every cutting point, two to three vertical shoots will grow, so factor that in and step back from the tree regularly to see the shape you're creating.

Prune above a bud

5
Keep going until the tree is your desired shape — you can prune back by around two-thirds, if needed. While this may look extreme, the tiny buds on the tree will spring into action and make it bushy again in just a few weeks.

63

WHAT YOU NEED

- Hedge trimmer, hand shears, or loppers
- Goggles
- Ladder

TECHNIQUE
How to prune an evergreen hedge

This is specifically for evergreen varieties, such as holly or privet. If you have a deciduous hedge, the same process can be carried out but should be done in late winter or early spring before the hedge comes to life.

WHY DO THIS NOW
By late spring or early summer the risk of frost has passed and there will be time for pruning cuts to heal before the heat of the summer.

BEFORE YOU START

- **Check for nesting birds** and postpone pruning if you do see any. In the UK, knowingly pruning when nesting birds are present is in violation of the Wildlife & Countryside Act 1981.

- **Wait until after the flowers have faded** if your evergreen hedge flowers in spring. Laurels are often best pruned in July or August.

- **Don't cut into old wood** unless the species can tolerate this. Check the RHS website or your local equivalent as a guide. For example, a yew hedge would be tolerant of this, whereas a leylandii would not.

- **Use hedge trimmers or shears** for most hedges. However, for large-leaved hedges, such as cherry laurel, it's best to prune individual stems with secateurs or loppers if you have the time — hand shears and trimmers can create cut leaf surfaces that look unsightly (don't worry if you don't have time though — you won't damage the plant).

1
Cut the hedge by sweeping the trimmer upwards. This will help you keep your balance, prevent you catching yourself in the leg, and help you get the right shape. If you're not using hedge trimmers, shape the hedge using your hand shears or loppers from the bottom and work your way up.

MAY

2
Trim the hedge into a wedge shape, with a slightly narrower top and wider bottom. This gives the whole plant the best opportunity for sunshine — perfect rectangles or wider-topped hedges will block the sun's rays from reaching the base of the plant. If the sun doesn't reach all the way to the bottom, you'll end up with patchy areas there.

3
Shape the top of the hedge as you like. If you want a flat top on your hedge, make horizontal cuts with the hedge trimmer. For rounded or shaped curves, slowly grade the cut down. Remember to step back frequently to get a good view of the overall shape.

WHAT YOU NEED

- Secateurs
- Drinking glass
- Pot
- Compost

TECHNIQUE
How to propagate plants in water

Propagating plants in water is a good method of starting new cuttings because you can easily keep an eye on root growth, you don't need to worry about watering, and for some plants it's quicker than propagating in soil. Water propagation is particularly great for softwood cuttings. This is the new, soft, and pliable growth which appears in spring.

WHY DO THIS NOW
Spring is when softer material is produced by plants, making it the perfect time to try this.

1
Take a cutting just below a leaf node and remove all the leaves except the top two.

2
Put the cutting in a glass of water in an area of bright, indirect light, and change the water regularly.

MAY

3
Wait until the plant has at least 5–7.5cm (2–3in) of roots, but no more than that, as it can become too acclimatized to water.

WHICH PLANTS CAN I PROPAGATE THIS WAY?

These plants are ideally suited to water propagation.

IVY   **MINT**

4
Prepare a pot with free-draining compost, create some holes, and gently plant the cuttings before backfilling. Keep the soil lightly damp but not soggy.

BASIL   **ROSEMARY**

GERANIUMS   **HYDRANGEAS**

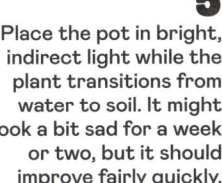 

5
Place the pot in bright, indirect light while the plant transitions from water to soil. It might look a bit sad for a week or two, but it should improve fairly quickly.

COLEUS   **WILLOW**

WHAT YOU NEED

- Secateurs

TECHNIQUE
How to deadhead roses for more blooms

Roses are one of those plants that require a little extra care. Later in the book I'll show you the right way to deadhead plants more generally (see pp.84–85), but there are two stages to deadheading roses. The first, which most people do, is purely aesthetic, but the second encourages blooms and helps to keep a compact shape.

WHY DO THIS NOW
Deadheading your roses in May encourages repeat flowering through the summer.

1
Remove the finished blooms from the flowering head. Pinch or cut off the finished flower just below the base of where it joins the stem. Leave any remaining buds or blooms to continue flowering.

2
To encourage more blooms, remove the entire flowering head once all the blooms in the cluster are finished. Roses come with leaves in sets of three or five. Remove the entire flowering head by cutting the stem at a 45-degree angle just above the first leaf with five leaflets.

MAY

WHAT YOU NEED
- Secateurs
- Hosepipe
- Mulch

TROUBLESHOOTING
How to treat roses with black spot

Black spot is a fungal disease that affects roses, appearing as unsightly black spots on their leaves, which then turn yellow, and are likely to fall off. If left, black spot can permanently damage the plant, but it's relatively easy to manage.

WHY DO THIS NOW
The disease often appears at this time of year when conditions are warm and wet, but if you deal with it now, the likelihood of future infections will be reduced. However, you can treat roses whenever you see signs of black spot on the leaves.

1
Remove any infected leaves, either with secateurs or by hand, pulling in the opposite direction to the growth. If you use secateurs remember to give them a good clean after to stop the spread of the disease.

2
Pick up any infected leaves that may have fallen to the ground, and either put them out with household waste or burn them. Do not put infected leaves in your compost heap because doing so will spread disease!

3
Mulch to a depth of around 5cm (2in) to lock in moisture (see pp.168–169) and stop fungal spores from splashing up onto the plant when watering. Water deeply to reduce stress on the plant, taking care not to water the foliage (see pp.20–21).

PRUNING
Pruning your rose at the right time (see pp.200–201) will reduce the chances of black spot, as well as other issues like mildew and mould, taking hold.

69

WHAT YOU NEED

- Scissors
- Twine or wire tie

TECHNIQUE
How to tie in climbing plants

Before you grab your twine and start tying away your climbing plants, take a moment to ask yourself: do you really need to? Some climbing plants are naturals and grow their own built-in climbing gear. Sweet peas, for example, send out tendrils that curl happily around anything nearby. Honeysuckle plants twist themselves around supports quite effortlessly. Ivy and Virginia creeper both have sticky little pads that stick to walls like tiny green pieces of Velcro. Wisteria, on the other hand, needs to be managed as its stems become large and woody.

WHY DO THIS NOW

For those plants that need tying in (such as tall perennials, trained shrubs, and fruit bushes) you should step in while the stems are still soft and bendy. In spring and summer, when growth is vigorous, you might find yourself tying them in almost weekly.

HELPING HAND
Remember that some climbers need a bit of nudging in the right direction. Don't be afraid to gently coax a shoot up its support or along the path you want it to follow. With a little patience and a soft touch, your climbers will happily wind their way to glory.

MAY

1
Cut the twine (**left**) or wire tie (**below**) to length and wrap once or twice firmly around the support and knot it. Loop it loosely around the plant stem and tie a couple of knots or twist to hold it without bruising. You can use either twine or wire tie for this job.

- **INCORRECT WAY**
- Tying the plant directly to the
- support will restrict its growth
- and damage the stem. It can also
- constrict or cut into the stem of
- the plant as it grows.

WHAT YOU NEED

- Hanging basket
- Coir, wool, or plastic liner
- Scissors
- Compost
- Plants
- Hosepipe

PROJECT
How to create a hanging basket

Hanging baskets are one of the easiest ways to squeeze plants into even the tiniest of spaces. Whether you hang them from a bracket by the front door, hook them up on the patio, or dangle a few along your balcony, they'll add instant colour and interest. You can go bold with colour in a sunny spot or pick plants that thrive in the shade. And they're not just for flowers like geraniums and pansies. Strawberries, tumbling tomatoes, and even a few herbs will happily grow in a basket.

WHY DO THIS NOW
Start your hanging baskets in May and you'll be able to enjoy them through the summer months.

1
Line your basket. Most baskets come with a liner already — usually coir (that fibrous coconut stuff) or plastic. If it's plastic, double-check it has drainage holes. If not, snip a few in with scissors so water can escape. If there is no liner, you can buy coir ones, cut up an old compost bag to fit, or place sheep's wool liners in the centre. Avoid moss unless you know it's sustainably harvested.

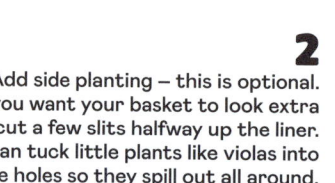

2
Add side planting — this is optional. If you want your basket to look extra lush, cut a few slits halfway up the liner. You can tuck little plants like violas into these holes so they spill out all around.

MAY

3
Add compost to the basket, then start planting your trailing plants around the edge, then pop taller or bushier ones in the centre. Fill in with compost, firming gently as you go, so there aren't any air pockets.

4
Give the basket a thorough soak and let it drain. This helps the compost settle in nicely around the roots.

AFTERCARE

FEED REGULARLY
Plants in baskets are packed in tightly and get hungry fast. Add a liquid feed to your watering can every couple of weeks to keep them blooming. Always water first, then feed, otherwise you risk damaging the roots.

KEEP UP WITH WATERING
Because baskets dry out quickly, especially in hot weather, you may need to water daily. The easiest way to check is to gently lift the basket – if it feels light, it needs a drink.

DEADHEAD OFTEN
Snip off faded flowers regularly and your plants will reward you with fresh blooms for weeks on end.

CHECK THE WEIGHT
Baskets are heavier than they look, once watered. Make sure the bracket or hook you're using is properly fixed and strong enough to hold the weight

WHAT YOU NEED

- Secateurs

TECHNIQUE
How to do the Chelsea chop

You might have heard gardeners talking about the "Chelsea Chop". It sounds fancy but it's just a clever pruning trick you can do in late May to early June (around the time of the RHS Chelsea Flower Show, hence the name). While it might feel a little brutal, it's worth doing. Your plants won't flop all over the place, they'll grow back bushier and sturdier, and you'll get flowers for longer over summer.

WHY DO THIS NOW
Late spring is a good time to prune plants that have grown since the winter but aren't too far into flower.

1
Choose from one of two methods shown here. Chop the whole plant back by 30–50 per cent (nepeta, **below**). You'll delay the flowering but end up with a neat, compact plant that won't keel over in summer.

Alternatively, cut back some of the plant, maybe the front section or every other stem (**above**). That way, the uncut sections flower first, and the cut stems follow later. This results in one plant with two blooming seasons. Give the plant some water if it's dry and maybe a little feed to help it bounce back. You'll soon see fresh new shoots coming up from below your cut.

MAY

MAKE A DISPLAY
Stick those cuttings in a vase indoors so that you can still benefit from the early blooms.

PLANTS TO CHELSEA CHOP

Not everything likes this treatment. Those listed below are perfect candidates for the chop.

ACHILLEA — ASTER
CAMPANULA — COREOPSIS
ECHINACEA — HELENIUM
HELIANTHUS — MONARDA
NEPETA — PENSTEMON
PHLOX — RUDBECKIA
SEDUM/HYLOTELEPHIUM — VERONICASTRUM

SUMMER

By summer, your garden is getting ready to really show off. Flowers are in full swing, borders are buzzing with bees, and every corner feels alive. Long, warm days mean plenty of time outside, but they also mean a lot of care and maintenance jobs will need to be done to ensure your plants stay healthy. Keep on top of deadheading, pruning, and watering and, most importantly, take the time to sit back and enjoy the garden at its peak.

JUNE

- **78** How to summer prune wisteria
- **80** How to prune climbing hydrangeas
- **82** How to grow a hedge
- **84** How to deadhead properly
- **86** How to set up a tropical garden
- **88** How to set up a compost bin
- **92** How to feed pots and hanging baskets
- **93** How to feed your lawn
- **94** How to grow herbs for the BBQ

JULY

- **96** How to protect plants in a heatwave
- **97** How to protect your garden hose in summer
- **98** How to deal with ants in your garden
- **100** How to take lavender cuttings
- **102** How to take semi-ripe hydrangea cuttings
- **104** How to plant strawberry runners
- **106** How to get a second flush of flowers

AUGUST

- **108** How to water your plants when you're on holiday
- **110** How to summer prune lavender
- **112** How to summer prune apple and pear trees
- **114** How to take semi-hardwood rose cuttings
- **116** How to reuse last year's compost
- **118** How to make a pallet planter
- **120** How to set up a water butt

WHAT YOU NEED

- Secateurs
- Scissors
- Twine

TECHNIQUE
How to summer prune wisteria

For a second flush of wisteria flowers, doing a summer prune in June after flowering as well as your winter prune (see pp.186–187) is essential. By this time of year your wisteria is likely a mass of leaves and whippy green shoots with seed pods popping up everywhere. Left to their own devices these whips will give you a lot of leaves but no flowers. Remove the seed pods at the same time and dispose of them carefully because they are poisonous to pets.

WHY DO THIS NOW
Pruning now will mean that the plant's energy will go into the flowers rather than leaves or seed pods. Wisteria also grows like crazy so pruning now will keep it from swamping fences, trellises, or pergolas.

New shoots

1 Use twine to tie any new green shoots into your support structure before starting so that you don't accidentally snip them off while pruning. Weave them through trellis or wrap them around posts.

SEED PODS
You should remove the seed pods because wisteria plants take 20 years to grow from seed, so you're unlikely to use them in this way. They're also poisonous to pets so you won't want them hanging around.

JUNE

The lumps where the leaves are coming out are the buds

2 Cut long vigorous shoots back at a 45-degree angle to around five buds from the base of the new growth. These are the shoots that you don't want to train. You can tell where the new growth starts as it's green compared to the older brown growth.

3 Cut off the seed pods to divert the plant's energy away from seed production to growing flowers.

Above Pruning in the correct way will ensure you get a beautiful display of flowers later in the summer.

79

WHAT YOU NEED

- Secateurs

TECHNIQUE
How to prune climbing hydrangeas

If you are comfortable with the size and shape of your climbing hydrangea then leave it alone. However, if the plant is very old or needs to be significantly cut back, you can do this process slowly over a few years, taking back a little bit more each time. That way you won't lose all your flower buds in one prune. Either way, go easy when pruning climbing hydrangeas. Most of the flower buds form near the top so you don't want to chop off too much.

WHY DO THIS NOW
Climbing hydrangeas flower on last year's growth, so if you need to prune them, do it in summer right after they've finished blooming so you have plenty of time to grow new shoots that'll carry next year's flowers.

1
Remove the faded flower heads and cut back any dead stems at a 90-degree angle.

OLD OR NEW WOOD
You can prune climbing hydrangeas on old or new wood, so just cut as needed to achieve the shape you're looking for.

JUNE

2
Shorten wayward shoots, always pruning just above two healthy buds. It may not be immediately obvious where to prune but look further back along the stem and you'll normally find two buds. This applies whether the wood is new (green) or old (brown).

3
Prune in the same way across the plant, and you'll have flowers next year.

WHAT YOU NEED

- Spade
- Potted plants or bare-root hedging
- Compost
- Hosepipe
- Bark chips

TECHNIQUE
How to grow a hedge

Growing a hedge as a border or garden divide is great, not only visually, as you get to grow more plants in place of a fence or wall, but because a hedge provides vital food and habitat for wildlife.

WHY DO THIS NOW

If you're using potted plants, now is a great time to do this so they can get established before the colder winter months. Bare-root hedging is available in winter or early spring when the plants are dormant so must be planted then.

1
Clear the area of any grass or weeds before you start as other plants will compete for water and nutrients. Next, dig the planting area. You can either dig a trench the full length of the hedge or individual holes slightly wider and deeper than the plant pots. If you're planting on a boundary, it is good practice to position a hedge between 0.5–1m (1.5–3ft) away from the boundary line.

JUNE

2
Place the hedging plants in your trench or holes, spacing them evenly along your hedge line. Check the spacing for your chosen plants. Almost all evergreen hedging can be planted into garden topsoil, but if your garden has heavy clay or sandy soil it's always a good idea to pack multi-purpose compost around the plants.

3
Position the roots at the same depth they were previously growing. If planting a bare-root hedge, you should still be able to see the soil line from when it was planted on the roots. Plant at or slightly above this level. Once in position, backfill the trench with soil, press firmly with your hands or feet to secure the plants, and water generously.

4
Mulch with bark chips to a depth of 7.5cm (3in) around your plants to help retain moisture and discourage weeds (see pp.168–169).

STAKING
Depending on the height of the hedge you may want to stake the plants, especially if they are in a high-wind area.

83

WHAT YOU NEED

- Secateurs

TECHNIQUE
How to deadhead properly

Most people know that the best way to prolong your blooms is to deadhead them. But many don't know how to do it properly. Just pulling off the petals isn't enough and won't give you the best results. Follow these steps to do it right.

WHY DO THIS NOW
If you pinch out flowers that have bloomed they won't expend energy on seed production, allowing your plant to focus on making new flowers instead.

Ensure you snip off entire seed head

USE SECATEURS
If you're using secateurs make sure that you are removing the flower head just above a healthy set of leaves or buds so the plant can put its energy into producing more blooms instead of seeds.

WHAT TO AVOID
Pinch or prune off the entire flower head rather than just pulling off the flower (**above**).

JUNE

FLOWERS THAT BENEFIT FROM REGULAR DEADHEADING

These flowers are all summer bloomers but the same rules apply for deadheading blooms throughout the year.

BEDDING PLANTS
Pinch off the flowers and stalks with your fingers for plants like argyranthemums, heliotropes, pansies, polyanthus, and petunias.

PELARGONIUMS
Pinch off the individual flowers first, then when the whole cluster has finished flowering, cut back to just above the main stem. Or you can just snap the stalk cleanly by pulling it down.

ROSES
Roses benefit from two stages of deadheading. Refer back to page 68 for how to do this.

SHRUBS
When you're deadheading rhododendrons, azaleas, camellias, lilacs, and tree peonies, snap or cut just below the flower head. Avoid removing new buds at the same time.

CLIMBERS
Get rid of spent flowers where you can reach them, especially on those that produce loads of seeds like *Eccremocarpus*. Cut near the base of each flower's stalk with your secateurs.

BULBS
For flowering bulbs like bearded iris, cut or pinch just behind where the seeds would form (just below the flower), but leave the green stalk alone — the bulb needs it to build up energy for next year's flowers.

WHAT YOU NEED

- Plants of your choice
- Compost
- Pots
- Mulch

PROJECT
How to set up a tropical garden

Everyone loves feeling like they're on holiday in their own garden, but finding tropical-style plants that can survive in a non-tropical environment can be difficult.

WHY DO THIS NOW

This is a great time to plant tropicals because the soil is warm, the days are long, and there's plenty of light for them to get established quickly. The heat encourages root growth, helping new plants settle in before the cooler months.

WHAT TO DO

- **Choose the right location** While many tropical plants like lots of bright, indirect sunlight, some prefer dappled light or shade, similar to the conditions of a rainforest, so check before planting. Think about where your plant will get the right light and remember that most tropicals aren't frost-hardy. Keeping them in pots makes it easy to bring them indoors or under cover during the winter months (see pp.144–145).

- **Prepare the soil** Use a rich, well-draining potting mix rather than garden soil, which can compact and hold too much water. Mulching the top (see pp.168–169) helps retain moisture, but make sure it doesn't sit right against the stem, which can encourage rot.

- **Select the right plants for the space** Plan for structure and colour. Pick large-leaved plants to give a bold backdrop and go for flowering plants to add pops of colour. Position taller palms or palms-like plants in the middle with medium-height shrubs around them and smaller plants or ground cover at the front to create layers.

- **Choose the right pot** Pick a pot that's large enough to accommodate root growth and has good drainage holes. Tropical plants do not like "wet feet", so drainage is crucial.

- **Gently loosen crowded or pot bound roots** Place the plant in the pot, fill in around it with potting mix, and firm lightly.

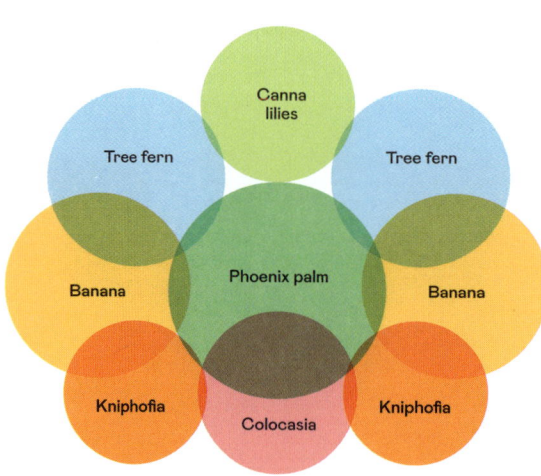

TROPICAL GARDEN PLANTING PLAN
These plants work well positioned in a circle with the taller palms in the centre. If you keep them in pots they can be moved as needed for protection over winter.

FIVE PLANTS TO GROW FOR A TROPICAL GARDEN

If you'd like to try to create your own little tropical paradise at home, here are five recommendations for plants to get you started.

MUSA BASJOO
The *Musa basjoo* is the hardiest of the banana plants. Growing to the size of a small tree, you can grow it in a pot or the ground in partial or full sun.

CANNA LILIES
Offering height and dramatic foliage, canna lilies are perfect for growing at the back or middle of a mixed or tropical border. This impressive tender perennial flowers through the summer and into autumn.

PHOENIX PALM
The semi-hardy *Phoenix* palm has deep green leaves and a stout trunk. Add some mulch to help with frost protection. During hot summers, it produces drooping bunches of creamy yellow flowers.

KNIPHOFIA
Also known as red hot pokers, kniphofia are not technically tropical but still give the right vibe with their amazing blooms in a range of fiery colours. Most species are hardy but there are some species that would need protection.

DICKSONIA ANTARCTICA
An incredible evergreen tree fern that's happy in shade. *Dicksonia antarctica*'s thick mass of roots form a trunk from which long fronds appear.

WHAT YOU NEED

- Compost bin
- Hosepipe
- Compost turning tool or aerator
- Worms (for setting up a wormery)
- Fork or spade

PROJECT
How to set up a compost bin

Composting is one of the simplest and most rewarding things you can do in the garden. It turns everyday kitchen scraps and garden clippings into rich, crumbly food for your soil, and all for free.

WHY DO THIS NOW

June is a great time to get a compost bin going. You'll have all those kitchen scraps, garden clippings, and the mountain of grass clippings from your lawn to break down and the natural heat accelerates the decomposition process.

WHAT IS COMPOST?

Good compost improves soil structure, helps it hold onto water, balances pH, and reduces plant diseases. It's packed with the key nutrients plants need — nitrogen, phosphorus, and potassium — while also making tricky soils (clay or chalk) a lot easier to work with. In short: compost makes your soil healthier, and healthy soil grows better plants.

COMMON METHODS

There are a number of ways to compost, which use roughly the same methods. These are the most common:

COMPOST HEAPS OR PILES
Just as it sounds — a simple heap left to rot down.

WORMERIES
Purpose-built containers where specialized worms do the hard work.

STANDARD BINS
The wooden or plastic bins you see in many gardens.

HOT COMPOSTERS
Insulated containers that break down waste quickly by trapping heat.

JUNE

1

Find the right spot. Put your compost bin or heap in a sunny-ish place, somewhere handy for tipping in scraps and scooping compost out later. If you're using a wormery, the container itself needs to be in contact with (or in) the ground so worms can move in and out.

FERMENTING WASTE
Bokashi composting uses anaerobic fermentation to break down food in a compost bin. It can be used for all types of food including meat and fish and is quicker than other methods, taking around two weeks to produce fermented waste. This then needs to be added to a compost heap or buried in soil before it can be used.

2

Save up uncooked fruit and veg peelings, teabags, eggshells, cardboard tubes, shredded paper, grass cuttings, and dry leaves. Skip cooked food, meat, or fish because they attract pests and don't break down well in most bins. Start with a base layer of brown materials, such as twigs, straw, or dry leaves, to help with drainage and airflow. Then alternate between:
- **Greens** – kitchen peelings, fresh grass cuttings, and plant trimmings.
- **Browns** – cardboard, shredded newspaper, and dry leaves.

Aim for roughly two parts brown to one part green waste, and if you're setting up a wormery, now is the time to add worms. You can't use earthworms – look for red wigglers, which are specialist compost worms available online.

3

Keep the heap damp (like a wrung-out sponge) and cover it if possible. Turn it every few weeks with a turning tool to add oxygen, which speeds things up.

89

4
Be patient. Good compost takes time – usually 9–12 months. Keep adding greens and browns as you go, and turn larger chunks over occasionally with a garden fork.

5
Check if it's ready. You'll know your compost is done when it looks dark and crumbly, smells earthy, and you can't recognize what went in (apart from the odd twig or eggshell).

6
Open the hatch at the bottom of your bin, or lift it slightly and scoop out the finished compost with a fork or spade when it's ready to use.

JUNE

7
Put it to use! Don't worry if it's a bit lumpy — that's normal. Spread it over borders, dig it into veg beds, use it as a mulch around shrubs, mix it into containers, or sprinkle it on the lawn as a natural feed.

TROUBLESHOOTING COMMON COMPOST PROBLEMS

MY COMPOST IS TOO DRY AND NOT ROTTING DOWN
Add more greens (veg peelings or grass clippings) and give it a light water to keep it damp like a sponge.

MY COMPOST IS TOO WET AND SLIMY
Add more browns (cardboard, straw, or dry leaves) to soak up the moisture and turn the heap to let in air.

FLIES OR PESTS ARE HANGING AROUND
Avoid putting in cooked food, meat, or dairy. If fruit flies are a nuisance, cover new scraps with a layer of browns each time.

THE COMPOST SMELLS BAD
This is usually a sign that it's too wet or contains too many greens. Balance it with browns, stir it through, and make sure there's drainage.

IT'S TAKING FOREVER
Chop materials smaller, turn the pile more often, and check the green-to-brown ratio. Warm conditions speed things up too.

WHAT YOU NEED

- Watering can
- Liquid or slow-release feed

TECHNIQUE
How to feed pots and hanging baskets

Plants growing in pots rely on you to keep them fed and watered. Most compost only contains enough nutrition to get them started, which runs out after about 6–8 weeks. After that, it's up to you to keep the food coming.

WHY DO THIS NOW
You're likely to have set up your hanging baskets and pots sometime in the spring so they will have run out of nutrition by now, so this is a good time to feed your plants to encourage more flowers.

WHAT KIND OF FEED?
If you're using liquid feed, mix it into a watering can as directed, and water your plants with it once a week or so. Liquid feeds are quick-acting and easy to control. Give each pot as much as you'd normally water it with. Think of it as replacing one of your daily waterings per week with a feed. Alternatively, slow-release fertilizer comes in pellets or capsules that you poke into the compost. They slowly release nutrients over weeks or months, so they're low maintenance.

CHOOSE THE RIGHT FEED
Match the feed to the plant. Use high-nitrogen feeds for leafy plants (this encourages lush green growth). Use tomato feed (diluted to half or quarter strength) for flowering plants to boost buds and blooms.

HOW OFTEN SHOULD I FEED?
Feeding too little or too much can cause harm. A heavy dose all at once can dehydrate plants (the salts pull water out of the roots), so steady, regular feeding is recommended. It may help to follow a routine. In spring, feed about once every two weeks. In summer, when plants are in full growth, increase to weekly feeds. For very hungry or fast-growing plants in big containers, feed twice weekly. Stop feeding at the end of summer to let plants wind down naturally.

LITTLE AND OFTEN
Feed little and often. Stick to regular small feeds and dilute liquid feeds exactly as the label says — more isn't better.

WATCH OUT FOR STRESS
Watch the plant's health. Don't feed plants that are already stressed (drooping from drought or recovering from root damage). Wait until they've perked up.

JUNE

WHAT YOU NEED
- Lawnmower
- Gloves
- Lawn fertilizer

TECHNIQUE
How to feed your lawn

Feeding your lawn is like giving it a balanced meal, it keeps the grass strong, green, and ready to face whatever the seasons throw at it. Do it right, and you'll swap patchy, tired turf for a thick, healthy carpet of green growth.

WHY DO THIS NOW
You can feed your lawn in spring and autumn but early June is still cool enough for the grass to take up nutrients without the fertilizer scorching the lawn in hot sun. A light summer feed now will green it up and keep it thick through dry spells.

1
Pick the right food for the right time, see box below.

2
Give the grass a trim so that the fertilizer makes contact with the soil.

3
Put on some gloves and apply the fertilizer when the grass is dry but the soil is damp. If the ground is parched, water it lightly the evening before so the soil has moisture, but the grass has time to dry.

4
Spread the feed on a cloudy day or in the evening to prevent the midday sun baking it in. Application depends on what type of feed you've chosen. Use a spreader for granular fertilizer or spread by hand for small patches. Many liquid feeds now come with hose attachments so you can spray them directly onto the lawn or use a watering can with a fine rose. Read the packet instructions. Overdoing these treatments can fry your grass.

WHICH FEED SHOULD I CHOOSE?
- **Spring feed** Go for something high in nitrogen (sometimes referred to as N). That's the nutrient that makes grass shoot up thick, lush, and green, perfect for getting the lawn looking sharp for summer.
- **Autumn feed** Choose a potash (sometimes referred to as K) heavy mix. Potash toughens up the roots, giving them armour for winter frosts.
- **Slow-release vs quick-release** Slow-release granules last for months but take a while to take effect. Quick-release or liquid feeds give instant results but need a careful hand (too much and you'll scorch the lawn).

WHAT YOU NEED

- Herbs of your choice
- Pots or herb planters
- Compost
- Watering can

PROJECT
How to grow herbs for the BBQ

Growing herbs to use in the kitchen or BBQ is a straightforward and worthwhile project. You can keep them on a windowsill or balcony if space is limited. Look for somewhere that gets plenty of sunlight and is sheltered and sunny. Plant them in well-drained soil and keep the soil moist but not overly wet and soggy.

WHY DO THIS NOW
This is prime BBQ season, so setting up a herb planter that's easily accessible to enhance your food will make eating outdoors a pleasure.

Left Not only are herbs super useful, but they're attractive plants that will happily grow in a variety of pot sizes.
Above A favourite of mine – BBQ peaches skewered with rosemary.

JUNE

FIVE GREAT HERBS TO GROW

All herbs are useful, but these are the ones that I think everyone should grow as they're versatile enough to be useful in a variety of dishes. They're great to grow in a container next to your BBQ area so you can pick and use them straight away.

BASIL
Easy to grow and attractive to pollinators, its strong aroma can be used in sweet and savoury dishes, and pairs well with tomatoes, pasta, and salads. Regular picking encourages more growth and it smells amazing.

SAGE
A hardy plant that will last for years. Like rosemary, this is an evergreen and keeps its soft silvery leaves all year round. It doesn't need constant pruning and is wonderful for stuffings and autumn vegetables.

THYME
A durable, drought-tolerant plant, requiring little maintenance once established. This aromatic herb is incredible in roasts, stews, and soups, and the tiny flowers are magnets for pollinators, especially bees.

ROSEMARY
A low-maintenance evergreen plant that can thrive in poor soil conditions and is long-lasting. Wonderful with potatoes, breads, and soups, it can also be dried easily or used fresh year-round.

PARSLEY
Easy to grow from seed, parsley is nutritious, tangy, and you can keep it going into winter if it's protected from frost. You can use this peppery herb in everything from salads to stews.

WHAT YOU NEED

- Watering can or hosepipe
- Pot mover or plant caddy (optional)
- Cloth or cardboard
- Stakes
- Mulch

TROUBLESHOOTING
How to protect plants in a heatwave

As summer temperatures become more unpredictable we're experiencing regular heatwaves. It's not difficult to help your plants out in times of extreme temperature, just follow these tips to give them all the support they need to thrive.

WHY DO THIS NOW
Take these steps during prolonged periods of extremely dry, hot weather and your plants will last for longer and stay healthy.

OUT OF THE SUN
Move any plants that you think may suffer in the sun.

WATER AT THE RIGHT TIME
When it's hot, the best time to water is early in the morning or later in the evening. Plants in containers should ideally be watered twice a day, as their soil will usually dry out more quickly than that in your beds.

MOVE POTS INTO SHADE
Potted plants will be the first to dry out in a heatwave, so you need to take extra care to ensure they do not perish during particularly hot spells. Place them in a shady spot where they are sheltered from the extreme heat of the midday sun. A pot mover or plant caddy can be useful when doing this.

CREATE SHADE
Plants suffering in borders can be protected with garden shades. A simple piece of cloth or cardboard fixed above them with stakes will provide some much-needed protection.

MULCH
Mulching helps plant roots retain moisture and can also keep the soil itself cool (see pp.168–169).

BE CAREFUL WITH FEEDING
If your plants need feeding during a heatwave, ensure that you do this at the right time. Fertilizer should never be added to dry soil, as this can lead to the plants becoming "burnt". Ideally, don't feed at all during a heatwave, but if you must, ensure the soil is kept moist to allow the nutrients to be properly absorbed.

JULY

WHAT YOU NEED
- Hosepipe
- Hose reel (optional)

TROUBLESHOOTING
How to protect your garden hose in summer

Your hose is your garden's lifeline, until it turns into a sun-baked, kinked-up nightmare. If you've ever gone to water the plants only to find your hose cracked, twisted, or leaking like a sieve, you're not alone. Luckily, with a couple of smart habits, you can keep it in top shape all summer long.

WHY DO THIS NOW
Summer is a risky time for your hose, as the hot weather can easily damage the rubber. Look after it now and you'll thank yourself next spring.

PREVENT YOUR HOSE FROM SPLITTING, CRACKING, OR KINKING
Always store your hose without any sharp bends or twists, especially during hot weather. Neatly looping the hose or using a reel with a controlled rewind function helps keep its shape intact and reduces stress on the rubber.

KEEP YOUR HOSE OUT OF DIRECT SUNLIGHT
Whenever possible, keep your hose out of the sun as extended UV exposure can dry out the material and cause it to crack. Using a reel with an enclosed case is a great way to shield it from the sun, but if you don't have that, just ensure that it's placed in a shady spot when not in use.

USE A HOSE REEL ON WHEELS
If your garden is large or awkwardly shaped, consider using a hose reel on wheels. That way, you can easily move the hose around, while still keeping it properly stored and shaded when not in use.

LOOK AFTER YOUR HOSE
Neatly loop your hosepipe to prevent it splitting in the summer.

WHAT YOU NEED

- Trowel, fork, or stick
- Hosepipe

TROUBLESHOOTING
How to deal with ants in your garden

Ants are an important part of garden biodiversity, and most of the time they don't cause direct harm to plants. Whenever possible, it's best to live alongside them, but when they set up home in the wrong place, such as in plant pots, compost bins, between patio slabs, or in the middle of your lawn, they can become a nuisance.

WHY DO THIS NOW
Ant colonies are most active in summer so you may only start to be aware of their nests around now.

FOR COMPOST BINS
If ants have taken over your compost bin, pop the lid on and let the temperature rise. Ants don't like hot, enclosed spaces and will usually relocate once things warm up inside.

BE WILDLIFE-FRIENDLY
Instead of reaching for boiling water, chemical sprays, or powders, which do more harm than good to the wider environment, use simple, wildlife-friendly ways to encourage ants to move on without killing them.

JULY

FOR POTS AND COMPOST HEAPS
Ants hate being disturbed. If they're nesting in a plant pot or compost heap, simply agitate the soil or compost every few days with a trowel, fork, or stick. The regular disruption will encourage them to move out.

FOR LAWNS AND PATIOS
Ants dislike damp conditions, so giving the area a regular soak with the hose will drive them away over time.

WHAT YOU NEED

- Secateurs
- Pot
- 50:50 mix of compost and horticultural grit
- Clear plastic bag

TECHNIQUE
How to take lavender cuttings

Taking cuttings can sometimes feel intimidating, but it is really simple to do, incredibly satisfying, and there's something a bit magical about turning one plant into many. Lavender is a great place to start and one of my favourite plants to propagate. Follow these steps and you'll have a garden that smells like a Mediterranean hillside in no time.

WHY DO THIS NOW
In July your plant will have fresh new shoots that won't yet have flowered, making them ideal for rooting. The warm weather also helps cuttings root quickly.

1
Select a straight and healthy lavender stem that doesn't have any flower buds. The best time to take a cutting is when the stem is just beginning to harden, showing a slight colour change from green to woody. Avoid using the old, fully woody part of the plant, as it won't root effectively. Snip the stem partway down, just above where it becomes fully woody. Aim for a length of around 10–15cm (4–6 in).

2
Once you have your cutting, gently strip off most of the leaves by running your fingers down the stem, leaving just a few leaves at the top.

JULY

Cut just below the leaf node

3
Prepare the base of the cutting by looking for a leaf node (the small bump or scar where a leaf once grew). Use a sharp knife to make a clean, straight cut just below this node.

4
Plant the cutting by gently pushing it into a pot filled with a 50:50 mix of compost and horticultural grit. Place cuttings around the outside of the pot, so they are supported.

5
Lightly mist the cuttings before covering with a clear plastic bag. Place the pot somewhere bright and warm but out of direct sunlight. Mist them once or twice a day being careful not to overdo it – lavender and other Mediterranean herbs don't like to sit in wet soil. After a while, you'll notice new leaves beginning to form. This is a sign that the cutting has rooted successfully, and you can pot it on into a larger container or plant it out in the garden.

WHAT YOU NEED

- Pot
- 50:50 mix of compost and horticultural grit
- Secateurs
- Clear plastic bag

TECHNIQUE
How to take semi-ripe hydrangea cuttings

Many gardeners struggle with their hydrangea cuttings wilting. But here's exactly how to do it right, with no wilt in sight.

WHY DO THIS NOW
New growth will be semi-ripe (not too soft and not too woody), making mid- to late summer the perfect time to do this. Cuttings taken earlier in the year will be more delicate.

1
Prepare a small pot filled with a 50:50 mix of multi-purpose compost and horticultural grit to ensure good drainage and aeration. It's important to get this ready first as cuttings rapidly dry out so you'll want to be able to move quickly. If you're taking a lot of cuttings keep a clear plastic bag nearby and put them in there. This will prevent excess water loss from their leaves.

2
Choose a straight, healthy hydrangea stem that has no flower buds. The stem should be around 15cm (6 in) long, or have three full sets of leaves. Count down three sets, then take your cutting just below the third leaf node.

Count down three sets of leaves and cut below the node

JULY

3
Remove all the leaves from the lower two-thirds of the cutting, leaving just the top two sets of leaves. Then, snip those remaining leaves in half to reduce water loss while the cutting roots.

4
Pot the cuttings around the edge of the pot. This gives them more support and better ensures they don't stay too soggy.

5
Give the cuttings a light mist of water, then cover the pot with a clear plastic bag, making sure it's not touching the leaves. This creates a humid environment, which is essential to stop the cuttings from wilting before they root.

6
Keep the pot in a warm, bright place out of direct sunlight, and mist lightly once a day. Once you see new leaf growth, you'll know your hydrangea cutting has taken root, and you've officially propagated your plant.

WHAT YOU NEED

- Pot
- Compost
- Strawberry runners
- Secateurs
- Jug or watering can

TECHNIQUE
How to plant strawberry runners

If you've ever been picking strawberries and spotted a little shoot snaking away from the main plant you've just found yourself a strawberry runner. That runner is basically a free strawberry plant waiting to happen.

WHY DO THIS NOW
Many strawberries make runners after they've finished fruiting in June.

1
Fill a small pot with multi-purpose compost. Nothing fancy needed, just make sure it drains well so the runner doesn't get soggy feet.

Look for a runner that already has a few leaves

2
Look for a runner that's already grown a few little leaves of its own. That's your clue it's ready to set down roots.

JULY

3
Set the runner gently on top of the compost. Use a bit of bent wire, a hairpin, or even a twig to hold it against the soil. Don't cut the runner's stem from the parent plant yet. It still needs that connection for food while it settles in.

4
Keep the compost moist but not waterlogged.

5
Give the new plant a gentle tug after a few weeks. If it resists, roots have formed. That's your green light to snip the stem linking it to the parent.

WHAT YOU NEED

- Secateurs
- Hosepipe

TECHNIQUE
How to get a second flush of flowers

Now is a great time to prune your perennials to get an extra burst of colour through mid to late summer, a technique also known as the "Hampton hack", as it's done around the time of the RHS Hampton Court Palace Garden Festival. As you'll see, it shouldn't take too long to do and will trigger another flush of blooms in your garden after the first cut has faded.

WHY DO THIS NOW
Doing this now will give your plants time before the end of the summer to burst into life again with a new flush of flowers.

1
Cut back any perennials that have finished flowering to around 10cm (4in) from the base. It might feel brutal, but don't worry, the plants can handle it.

2
Give everything a generous soak and feed to help them recover. Within a week or two, you'll see new, healthy growth starting to emerge.

EARLY VARIETIES
This technique works best on early flowering varieties, such as *Geranium sylvaticum*, *G. endressii*, and *G. phaeum* or salvias such as 'Mainacht' and 'Blauhügel' as they will have time for a second flush of flowers before the end of the season.

JULY

PLANTS THAT ARE PERFECT FOR THE HAMPTON HACK

ACANTHUS

ALCHEMILLA MOLLIS

BRUNNERA

CENTRANTHUS

DELPHINIUM

GERANIUM SYLVATICUM

LUPINS

MINT

MONARDA

ORIENTAL POPPIES

SALVIA 'MAINACHT'

VERONICA

WHAT YOU NEED

- Bucket
- Twine
- Scissors
- Stones or rocks to use as weights

PROJECT
How to water your plants when you're on holiday

There's nothing worse than coming back from holiday to wilted flowers. What I'm about to suggest will not beat an automatic watering system, but if you don't have one this will help. With just a bucket, some string, and a rock, you can make a simple DIY watering system that will keep your plants happy while you're away.

WHY DO THIS NOW
It's a good idea to do this anytime you're away over summer, and August is prime time for a summer holiday!

1
Fill a bucket with water.

2
Cut lengths of string long enough to reach from your plant pots to a raised area above them (such as a table). Soak them in the bucket until fully saturated.

108

AUGUST

3
Tie one end of each length of string around a rock, then drop it into the bucket.

4
Position the bucket higher than your plants, then push the other end of each piece of string into the soil of a pot. The string will act as a wick, drawing water from the bucket into the compost whenever it starts to dry out, keeping your plants watered without you lifting a finger.

WHAT YOU NEED

- Secateurs

TECHNIQUE
How to summer prune lavender

Don't leave this one too late gardeners, your lavender is practically begging for a haircut by August. Some people prefer to prune lavender in the autumn, but the timing should be dictated by the plant rather than the season, you'll know when it needs doing.

WHY DO THIS NOW

Pruning now when the lavender's flowers are just beginning to fade gives the plants time to create a small amount of new growth, which will protect them when the colder temperatures arrive.

1
Here you can see two lavenders of the same variety side by side. The one just going past its best is ready to prune, the one in full bloom isn't. Don't wait until the flowers are brown or going to seed, catch them while they're fading.

AUGUST

2
Look closely at your lavender and find the spot just above the old wood where fresh new shoots are sprouting. Take the plant in manageable handfuls and begin cutting back at a 90-degree angle to just above those new growth points. Cut back quite hard — as long as you leave some green, new growth below your cutting point the plant will be fine.

Prune just above the old wood

3
Shape the plant into a tidy, rounded mound. Don't cut into old wood (the woody, brown stems near the base) as these may not regrow and this can weaken or even kill the plant.

WHAT YOU NEED

- Secateurs

TECHNIQUE
How to summer prune apple and pear trees

When your apple or pear tree is throwing out big leafy shoots in summer, it can be tempting to just chop away at them. But a little know-how goes a long way. Pruning properly stops long shoots getting out of hand (trust me, they'll double in length if left alone), helps light and air reach ripening fruit, and encourages the tree to put its energy into fruit buds instead of just more leaves.

WHY DO THIS NOW
Proper pruning now will control the size of the tree and improve fruit production.

1
Look for those long, whippy shoots shooting up from the main branches. They'll usually be covered in big leaves and can feel a bit wild compared to the rest of the tree.

WHY PRUNE TWICE?
When you prune in the winter it is to stimulate growth, remove dead and crossing branches, and create the tree's structure. Pruning in the summer helps control growth, manage the tree's size, improves the quality of the fruit, and reduces the risk of disease.

AUGUST

2

Follow each shoot down towards where it started growing this year. You'll notice a cluster of leaves right at the base. That's the start of this season's growth.

3

Count three or four buds up the stem from that leafy base. That's your cutting point. Snip at an angle just above that third or fourth bud.

Cluster of leaves at the shoot base

Snip at an angle just above the bud

Next year's fruit will grow from spurs like this

- **DON'T TOUCH THE SPURS**
- Those stubby, short shoots packed with tight little leaves? Leave them be!
- They're fruiting spurs, and that's where next year's apples and pears will
- grow. Cutting those off is like throwing away next season's harvest.

WHAT YOU NEED

- Secateurs
- Pot
- 50:50 mix of compost and horticultural grit
- Water spray
- Clear plastic bag

TECHNIQUE
How to take semi-hardwood rose cuttings

You love your roses? Of course you do. The good news is that now is a great time to take cuttings so that you can have more of them. Taking semi-hardwood rose cuttings is much easier than taking softwood cuttings as they are much less likely to wilt – which means more roses for less stress.

WHY DO THIS NOW
Late summer to early autumn is a great time to take cuttings from semi-hardwood rose plants as this is when you can find stems that are not green or hardwood but something in between.

1
Look for a stem that's neither too soft nor too hard. Avoid the very top, which is still bendy softwood, and look further down until you find a section that's firmer, but not yet woody. That's your sweet spot: semi-hardwood.

First cut on a 45-degree angle

Second cut at a 90-degree angle

2
Make your first cut on a 45-degree angle just above a bud. Then measure down about 10–15cm (4–6in) and make a second cut at a 90-degree angle below a bud. This helps you easily remember which end is the top and which is the bottom.

AUGUST

3
Prepare your pot — a 50:50 mix of compost and horticultural grit offers drainage. Remove all the leaves from the cutting except for the top two. Cut those remaining leaves in half to reduce water loss.

4
Remove any thorns that might get in the way of handling or planting by pushing them off at a right angle.

5
Repeat this process for any additional cuttings and place them evenly around the edge of the pot, not in the centre.

6
Mist the cuttings with water and then cover the pot with a clear plastic bag to maintain humidity while the roots develop.

WHAT YOU NEED

- Tray
- Trowel
- Fertilizer
- Compost or well-rotted manure

TECHNIQUE
How to reuse last year's compost

We've all been there, you reach for your pots, and they're still full of last year's compost and dead plants. The temptation is to throw it all out and start fresh, but you really don't need to. Old compost can be given a second life, saving you money and cutting down on waste.

WHY DO THIS NOW
Doing this now means you can reuse the compost from your spring displays in your summer and autumn pots.

1
Start by tipping out the compost into a tray and removing any weeds, old roots, plant matter, and stones (you can add them to your compost heap). Break up any big clumps with a trowel so the compost is nice and crumbly.

2
Mix in a handful or two of general-purpose organic fertilizer, like a scoop of slow-release feed.

AUGUST

3
Add some fresh compost or well-rotted manure to liven it up. One part fresh to two parts old is a good rule of thumb.

4
Give everything a good mix so the old and new composts blend together evenly. You'll end up with a revived compost that is perfect for topping up pots or filling raised beds.

- **WHEN NOT TO REUSE**
- If plants grown in the compost showed signs of disease or mildew, don't risk re-using it as you'll pass the disease on to the next plants you place it in.
- Similarly, if you see pests in the compost it's best to dispose of it.

WHAT YOU NEED

- Safety goggles
- A wooden pallet
- Hammer
- Sandpaper
- Saw or jigsaw
- Crowbar or reciprocating saw
- Screwdriver or drill with screwdriver bits
- Wood screws
- Landscaping fabric or old compost bags
- Nails or strong adhesive

PROJECT
How to make a pallet planter

Deep planters hold more water, give roots space to spread, and keep plants happier all round, but they can be expensive. It's possible to make your own in about an hour from a wooden pallet and a few tools. When choosing a pallet, look for the "HT" stamp for heat-treated wood; avoid any marked MB (methyl bromide) as this is a toxic fumigant that isn't suitable for gardens.

WHY DO THIS NOW
Now is great as you're probably looking for more excuses to spend time in the garden and a pallet planter is ideal for growing herbs and flowers.

1
Before you start, give the pallet a once-over. Pull out or hammer in any nails that are sticking out, sand off big splinters, and make sure it's solid enough to cut up without collapsing.

2
Divide the top of the pallet into three equal sections across its width. Cut along those lines with a saw or jigsaw without cutting all the way through to the back. This will give you the three sections to use for the bottom and sides of your planter.

3
Now turn the pallet over, remove the slats from the back, and put them to one side to use in step 5. You could use a crowbar to get the slats off or loosen them with a hammer and use a reciprocating saw with a metal cutting blade to cut through the nails.

AUGUST

4

Your pallet should now come apart into three sections. Flip the middle piece over to form a base and turn the outside pieces to form the sides. Make sure everything is positioned correctly then screw the pieces together.

5
Fill in gaps in the side using the spare pieces of wood. Cut some lengths in half and screw them into place at each end of your planter.

6
Position the planter where you want it while it's empty as once filled, it'll be too heavy to move. Line the inside with landscaping fabric or old compost bags. This stops soil from washing out through the cracks and helps retain moisture. Attach it with nails, or a strong adhesive that is suitable for outdoors.

7
Fill the planter with compost and get planting. Whether you go for veg, herbs, or bold bedding, you've got yourself a big new container for next to nothing, and the satisfaction of knowing you built it yourself.

119

WHAT YOU NEED

- Water butt
- Drill and drill bit
- Diverter kit
- Spirit level
- Scribing tool or knife
- Hacksaw
- Watering can

PROJECT
How to set up a water butt

A water butt diverts and captures rainwater from your downpipe. The rain still comes off the roof into the gutter, but instead of disappearing down the pipe, a little diverter guides it into your butt. When the butt is full, any extra water simply carries on down the drain like usual. You can buy water butts and diverter kits from most garden centres or online.

WHY DO THIS NOW
Setting up a water butt before autumn means you get to capture all the rain that's about to fall, creating a free natural water supply for the coming season.

1
Many water butts have pre-drilled holes but if yours doesn't, drill a hole about 10cm (4in) from the top (your diverter kit will tell you the right diameter, usually around 26mm or 1in). Push the hose connector through from the inside, then tighten it up with the washer and nut on the outside.

2
Place the butt next to the downpipe (no more than 50cm/20in away) and mark out a section where the diverter will sit. Use a spirit level to make sure the diverter will be level with the top of the water butt and make a mark on the downpipe with your scribe or knife.

AUGUST

4
Attach the flexible hose from the butt to the connector on the downpipe. Make sure it's snug so nothing leaks. To test it, pour a watering can down the gutter — if it flows into the butt, you're good to go.

3
Cut through the downpipe at that mark with your hacksaw (**above**) and insert the diverter into the gap. You may need to slightly trim the bottom section of your downpipe to fit the diverter. This will vary depending on your diverter (**below**).

MAKE A WATER FEATURE OF IT
If you have a standard water butt, keep the lid on to stop leaves and other muck falling in. If you fancy making more of a feature of your water butt, you can add a bubbler or other water feature. Not only does it look good, but moving water keeps mosquitos away (they prefer stagnant water to breed in).

AUTUMN

Some plants and flowers may be winding down a bit as autumn begins, but the garden is far from finished. Colours shift to rich reds, oranges, and golds, and late-flowering plants give one last burst before winter sets in. It's a season of change, and a good time to take stock and prepare for next year's growing season. Autumn can actually be a busy time for gardeners, so prioritize activities that will help your garden prepare to rest, while quietly setting the stage for next year's show.

SEPTEMBER

124 How to level a lawn
126 How to treat leatherjackets
128 How to plant hyacinth bulbs for Christmas
130 How to prepare your garden furniture for storage
132 How to layer spring bulbs in pots
134 How to plant pots for autumn colour

OCTOBER

136 How to look after your plants in autumn
138 How to store seeds
140 How to make leaf mould
141 How to set up a log store
142 How to plant bulbs in your lawn
143 How to prepare your greenhouse for winter
144 How to prepare tropical plants for winter
146 How to make a bug hotel
148 How to plant amaryllis bulbs for a Christmas display

NOVEMBER

150 How to plant spring bulbs in a border
152 How to prepare your garden hose for winter
154 How to insulate outdoor taps
155 How to do the last mow of the year
156 How to keep your pots tidy with an old pair of tights
158 How to protect pots from frost
160 How to prepare borderline hardy plants for winter
162 How to prepare your garden tools for winter
164 How to plant paperwhites for a Christmas display
166 How to care for ponds over winter
168 How to mulch

WHAT YOU NEED

- Lawnmower
- Topsoil, sand, and compost mix
- Spade
- Rake or levelling rake
- Hosepipe
- Grass seed (optional)

TECHNIQUE
How to level a lawn

If your lawn has taken a few knocks over the summer and has some lumps and bumps, it's time to take action. This is a job that can be done now or in the spring. You can follow these steps for smoothing out small divots and bumps of around 2–3cm (¾–1in).

WHY DO THIS NOW
The soil is still warm and the temperatures are mild and there is usually enough rainfall for the revived areas to become established before winter sets in.

1
Start by preparing the area. Mow your lawn to around 2–3cm (¾–1¼in) in height. This gives you a clear view of uneven areas and makes it easier for your top-dressing mix to settle in. Make your mix by combining two parts topsoil, two parts sand, and one part compost. This blend gives you the ideal balance of structure, drainage, and nutrients to support healthy grass growth.

FOR LARGER AREAS
This method is ideal for minor dips up to 3cm (1in) deep. If your lawn is extremely bumpy, then you'll need to lift your turf and build the ground level up again before re-laying the turf.

SEPTEMBER

2
Apply the mix across the lawn with a spade, focussing especially on the low or uneven spots.

3
Once down, use the back of a rake or a levelling rake to spread the mix evenly across the surface.

4
Firm it in gently by walking up and down the lawn. If necessary, repeat the process in areas that still need raising up by adding more top-dressing. Finish by watering the lawn lightly to help the mix settle and bond with the existing soil. If the lawn is sparse or patchy, you can now overseed (see pp.48–49).

WHAT YOU NEED

- Cardboard or black plastic sheeting
- Nematodes
- Watering can

TROUBLESHOOTING
How to treat leatherjackets

If your once-green lawn is suddenly patchy, weak, and looking more like a moth-eaten jumper than a lush carpet, you might have uninvited guests — leatherjackets, the larvae of daddy longlegs. A few leatherjackets in your lawn is not the end of the world and can act as a food for wildlife. However, an infestation can lead to dead patches in the lawn, thinning grass, and even the complete loss of a lawn.

WHY DO THIS NOW
Late summer into autumn is the perfect time to strike because this is when the leatherjackets are small and most vulnerable. Treating your lawn at this time of year also means it's still warm enough for the nematodes to be effective.

CRANEFLY LARVA
Leatherjackets are fat, grey-brown grubs with no legs.

1
Check whether you have leatherjackets by watering the lawn thoroughly, covering a patch with cardboard or black plastic sheeting, and leaving overnight. If you spot the fat, grey-brown grubs on the surface when you remove the cover, you've found your problem. Doing this alone will help you to deal with light infestations as you can pick off the grubs. For larger areas you'll need nematodes (see box on the best treatment, **opposite**).

SEPTEMBER

- **THE BEST TREATMENT**
An effective way to treat leatherjackets is with nematodes. These microscopic worms actively hunt down the larvae in the soil. Make sure to use nematodes specifically for this species of larvae as there are different types to target different pests. For persistent problems you may need to repeat the treatment.

2
Following the pack instructions, mix the nematodes with water in a watering can.

Nematodes come in a powdery form like this

3
Apply the mixture evenly over the affected lawn. Make sure you keep the lawn watered, as the nematodes need moist conditions to work effectively.

- **ATTRACT NATURAL PREDATORS**
Aim to prevent the problem in the first place by attracting predators to your garden. Birds like starlings, rooks, and crows will pick up grubs if you rake your lawn and bring them to the surface.

127

WHAT YOU NEED

- Compost
- Pot or bulb vase
- Hyacinth bulbs
- Watering can
- Sphagnum moss (optional)

PROJECT
How to plant hyacinth bulbs for Christmas

Garden centres sell blooming hyacinth displays at Christmas but if you want to grow them from bulbs yourself, you've got until the end of September to get started so that you have blooms for the latter part of December. These fragrant flowers make beautiful festive displays and you can grow them in pots or in water.

WHY DO THIS NOW
Planting your hyacinth bulbs in early to mid-September should give you blooms in time for Christmas. If you wait until October your hyacinths will flower in the New Year.

1
Add a 5cm (2in) layer of compost to the bottom of your pot, then place the bulbs in the compost with the pointy bits sticking up. Position them close together without touching.

2
Fill in around them so the top half of each bulb is still visible, then lightly water the compost.

- **PREPARED BULBS**
- Whichever method you choose, use prepared hyacinth bulbs rather than ordinary bulbs, which won't bloom on schedule. Prepared bulbs have already had a period in the cold to encourage early flowers.

SEPTEMBER

3
Top with sphagnum moss. It's optional but makes the display prettier and prevents splashing when watering.

4
Place the pot in a cool, dark spot for around 10 weeks until shoots appear. At that point, move them into a light, airy place to bring on the flowers right in time to brighten up your Christmas.

USING A BULB VASE

For this method you'll need a bulb vase with a rounded base, long neck, and cupped shape at the top – a normal vase won't work. Fill the vase with water to just below the neck so the bulb doesn't touch the surface. Then pop the bulb in the neck of the vase, with the pointy end facing up. Over the coming weeks, roots will grow down towards the water. Leave the vase in a cool, dark spot for around 10 weeks until shoots appear. At that point, move it into a light, airy place to bring on the flowers.

WHAT YOU NEED

- Soft brush
- Bucket
- Washing-up liquid
- Hosepipe
- Sponge
- Sandpaper (for wooden furniture)
- Outdoor wood oil or preservative (for wooden furniture)

TECHNIQUE
How to prepare your garden furniture for storage

A big part of garden care is preventative work. So don't let your garden furniture face winter unprepared. A little care now can save you from a sorry, weather-beaten mess come spring. It's a good idea to clean patios or stonework at the same time to reset them after the summer (see pp.58–59).

WHY DO THIS NOW
Get these jobs done before the first frost and your furniture will be ready to roll out again the moment the sun returns.

1
Use a soft brush to remove dust and debris from furniture frames and leaves, dirt, and grime from cushions.

WOODEN FURNITURE
If you have wooden chairs and tables outside, sweep off any leaves and muck, then wash them with warm, soapy water to shift mildew and grime. Leave to dry and then sand any rough patches. A coat of outdoor wood oil or a decent preservative will help keep the damp out and stop cracking. If you can, stash the furniture in a shed or garage, or pop on a breathable cover and put a couple of bricks under the legs so it's not sitting in water over the winter.

SEPTEMBER

2
Gently wash outdoor cushions and tables using washing-up liquid, water, and a sponge. Make sure they are totally dry before storing them indoors to prevent mould and mildew from taking hold, as well as any damage from freezing temperatures.

3
Brush down synthetic outdoor rugs with clean water and make sure they are fully dry before you pack them away.

WHAT YOU NEED

- Compost
- Pot
- Trowel
- Bulbs
- Watering can

TECHNIQUE
How to layer spring bulbs in pots

With a little planning, you can create a layered bulb display that bursts into colour in early spring and keeps going right through to summer. Here's how to stack your "bulb lasagne" for a continuous burst of colour from March to June.

WHY DO THIS NOW
Planting in September gives bulbs time to establish their roots before the frost bites and a spell of cold weather triggers flowering in the new year. However, if you want to include tulips in your pot it's best to wait until late October as the cooler weather helps to stop a fungal disease called tulip fire.

1
Place a layer of compost in the bottom of your pot and plant the largest, latest-flowering bulbs, such as alliums and tulips, first. Place them at a depth of around 15–25cm (6–10in) and cover them with a layer of compost. There should be 5–7.5cm (2–3in) of compost between each layer.

2
If you're planting two sets of mid-season bloomers, such as daffodils and hyacinths, plant one 15cm (6in) deep and the other 10cm (4in) deep to create another layer.

SEPTEMBER

BULB PROTECTION
If you live somewhere with pests that will dig up your bulbs you could cover the pot with some chicken wire for protection. You can also cover the bulbs with chilli powder or flakes to deter them.

3
Finish with early risers, such as crocuses, winter aconites, and snowdrops, at a shallower depth of 5–10cm (2–4in).

4
Cover everything with a final layer of compost and water.

WHAT YOU NEED

- Plant pots or hanging baskets
- Compost
- Trowel
- Plants of your choice

PROJECT
How to plant pots for autumn colour

Empty pots in autumn are a missed opportunity. Just because summer's blooms have faded doesn't mean your containers have to sit bare until spring. With the right plants, you can keep the colour and texture going well into winter. I love bold autumnal colour schemes, with single-tone plantings in white, red, or green standing out beautifully in containers and looking just as striking in hanging baskets. It's completely up to you, but there's no need to stop gardening now.

WHY DO THIS NOW
As your summer blooms fade, this is the perfect time to add a pop of colour to your garden that will take you into the winter months.

FOR HANGING BASKETS
Here a handful of cyclamen adds a pop of colour to the basket that also contains calocephalus, and trailing ivy over the edge for a wilder feel.

FOR POTS
Try to get a balance of foliage plants with some height, such as heather and calocephalus, and flowers like cyclamen for colour.

SEPTEMBER

FLOWERING PLANTS FOR AUTUMN

VIOLAS AND PANSIES
You can't beat violas or pansies in deep jewel shades. Pair them with ornamental cabbage or kale, and let creeping thyme or trailing heather spill over the edge of your pot.

CHRYSANTHEMUMS
With daisy-like flowers and dense clusters of petals, chrysanthemums come in a variety of strong colours, including yellow, pink, purple, and white.

CYCLAMEN
With flowers in colours including white, pink, and red, the delicate cyclamen has heart-shaped leaves.

ASTERS
Asters are a great choice for autumn pots as they come in a range of bright colours and are long-lasting.

FOLIAGE PLANTS FOR AUTUMN

HEATHERS
Add long-lasting texture and soft colour with heathers. They keep their structure even through frost.

CONIFERS
Provide evergreen height and shape with dwarf conifers that also give pots year-round structure and a focal point.

IVY
Add trailing greenery and soften container edges with ivy that will stay lush through autumn and winter.

GRASSES
Add structure and texture to your pots with grasses such as *Festuca glauca* (**left**), *Stipa tenuissima*, and *Miscanthus sinensis*. A splash of black mondo grass adds drama and interest.

WHAT YOU NEED

- Secateurs
- Paper bag or envelope

TECHNIQUE
How to look after your plants in autumn

It can be difficult to know what's best for your garden in the autumn. Should you cut everything down or leave it as it is? There are few hard and fast rules. I love the silhouettes that are left behind by plants like hydrangea as they give the garden structure and interest when most plants have finished blooming. This is also the time to collect seeds or leave them either to self-seed or for wildlife to enjoy. Here are some suggestions for what you can do with your fading plants.

WHY DO THIS NOW
It's a good time to collect seeds for next year and decide whether to cut plants back or leave them for a structural look.

ENCOURAGE SELF-SEEDING
Brush your hand gently over dead flower heads like echinops (**left**) to shake loose seeds, which will scatter into the soil. Many plants, such as poppies, foxgloves, and nigella are brilliant self-seeders. By letting nature do the work, you can get a free carpet of seedlings popping up next spring, without lifting a finger.

WHAT TO CUT BACK
A lot of perennials like asters, echinacea, rudbeckias, grasses, and sedums look lovely left standing through winter. Their seed heads look great when frosted, adding a bit of texture and structure, while the hollow stems give insects somewhere to hide and the seeds feed hungry birds. So don't feel you have to cut everything back, leaving things be is often the best move. That said, anything that turns to mush after a frost, like hostas or dahlias, is worth clearing once it collapses.

OCTOBER

COLLECT SEEDS
Snip off the seed heads of plants like eryngium (**below**) and shake or tease out the seeds into a paper bag or envelope (see pp.138–139). Some seeds, like agapanthus, are better sown fresh, so don't be afraid to plant a few straight away.

LEAVE PLANTS FOR BIRDS
Sometimes the best option is simply to leave the dead stems standing. They might look a bit scruffy, but to birds like goldfinches, they're an all-you-can-eat buffet. Plants like echinacea (**above**) and rudbeckia hold onto their seeds right through the colder months, offering both food and shelter. Plus, their dried shapes catch the frost and look beautiful in the low winter sun.

WHAT YOU NEED

- Secateurs
- Paper bag
- Sheet of paper
- Envelope
- Pen or pencil
- Silica gel
- Airtight container

TECHNIQUE
How to store seeds

Garden centre plants can be expensive, usually because they've taken months to grow, but it does sting when you're filling a trolley. The good news is, a lot of the time we can get plants for free, just by collecting seeds from our own gardens.

WHY DO THIS NOW
Late summer and autumn are the perfect times to do this, as it's when lots of plants are setting seed.

1
Snip off the seed heads, turn them upside down into a bag, and let the seeds drop in. You don't need anything fancy, just a paper bag will do.

2
Keep the bag in a cool, dry place for a couple of weeks and the pods will dry out and release the rest of the seeds. You can pull them gently apart to help this process.

OCTOBER

3
Tip everything onto a sheet of paper, give the seed heads a tap to get out the last few stragglers, then fold the paper so you can pour the seeds into an envelope.

4
Label the envelope clearly — you'll never remember what you have by spring — and seal it up.

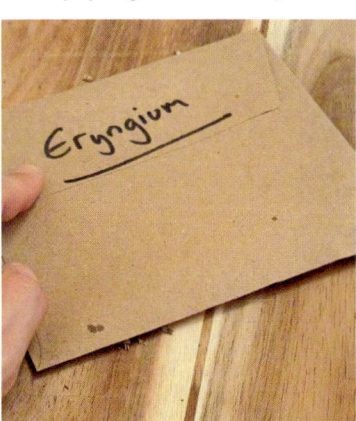

5
Store your seeds with care. Tuck the envelopes into an airtight container with a little packet of silica gel to keep them dry, and put it into the salad drawer of the fridge. Don't leave them on a sunny windowsill, in a steamy kitchen drawer, or anywhere damp because they'll lose their oomph. When spring rolls around those seeds will be ready to sprout like they've just fallen fresh from the plant.

WHAT YOU NEED

- Plastic bag
- Watering can or hosepipe
- Pen or pencil

TECHNIQUE
How to make leaf mould

Leaf mould forms when leaves break down slowly through fungal activity, rather than the fast, hot, sometimes smelly bacterial process of composting. This produces a rich, crumbly soil conditioner that's fantastic for improving structure and water retention.

WHY DO THIS NOW
Now is a good time to start making your own supply of leaf mould ready for mulching next year or the year after.

1
Gather up fallen leaves into a plastic bag. There are often pre-packed bags at this time of year as the council starts to clear away all the fallen leaves in the area. Check first, but if they're happy for you to take them, then this step is done for you!

2
Make sure the leaves are damp (add a splash of water if needed), then tie the top of the bag securely. To speed up the leaf mould creation process you can shred the leaves first but there's no need to do this if you're happy to wait a little longer.

3
Use a pen or pencil to poke a few holes in the bottom of the bag so excess water can drain away.

4
Store the bag somewhere shady out of the way and forget about it. In around one or two years, you'll open it to find some beautifully broken-down leaf mould, ready to use as mulch in your garden (**right**).

WHICH LEAVES ARE BEST FOR THIS?
- **Oak, beech, and hornbeam** These break down quickly and make excellent-quality leaf mould, so the steps given here are all you need.
- **Sycamore, walnut, horse chestnut, and sweet chestnut** These thicker leaves will decompose more slowly; shred them before adding them to the bag.
- **Pine needles** If you can, keep these separate to make acidic leaf mould — perfect for mulching rhododendrons, azaleas, camellias, pieris, and blueberries.

OCTOBER

WHAT YOU NEED

- Log store

PROJECT
How to set up a log store

An effective log store keeps your firewood dry and ready to burn all winter. Whether you're buying one or building your own, getting the details right will make all the difference to how long it lasts and how well it works.

WHY DO THIS NOW

Setting up your log store now means freshly cut logs can start seasoning (the process of drying out for use on a fire) for next year and wood that is already seasoned is kept dry and ready to burn.

1
Material is important. Choose treated timber with a weather-resistant finish so it can withstand year-round exposure. Without this, your store will quickly deteriorate in the elements.

2
Go for the largest store you can fit. A half-full store is never a problem, but running out of space for logs in winter definitely is.

3
Ideally, place the store on a level concrete base and elevate it so the wood isn't sitting directly on the floor. Slats in the bottom will also elevate the wood.

4
Check for good airflow all round. Side gaps or slats allow air to circulate freely around the logs. Avoid enclosed designs with doors that trap humidity and encourage mould and pests.

5
Look for a forward-sloping roof, taller at the back than the front to keep out rain and snow while protecting your logs. If it's positioned against a wall, this design also helps prevent damp from creeping into your home.

WHAT YOU NEED

- Spring bulbs
- Spade
- Watering can

TECHNIQUE
How to plant bulbs in your lawn

Having bulbs appear in the lawn is one of those magical garden moments. Crocuses peeking through in February, daffodils bobbing in March, fritillaries nodding in the damp grass... it looks so natural, as if they just decided to grow there on their own. The good thing is, getting bulbs to grow without wrecking your grass is not as hard as you might think.

WHY DO THIS NOW
Bulbs for spring are best planted now before the ground is frozen to allow them to grow their roots and because they need a cold snap before they flower.

1
Aim for natural, not neat. Bulbs always look best when they're planted in drifts, not in soldier-straight rows. Toss them gently into the air and plant them where they land. That scatter gives you the relaxed, meadow-like effect you're after. Stick to one variety in a patch — say, just crocus or just daffodils — for a bold sweep of colour that feels intentional rather than messy.

2
Push your spade firmly down into the grass once and then again to make a cross shape. Aim for around 2–3 times the depth of the bulb, so 5cm (2in) deep for smaller bulbs like crocus, and 10–15cm (4–6in) for daffodils. Next, put the spade into the ground just behind the cross and pull back on the handle gently. This should open up the cross so you can easily pop the bulbs in.

3
Place one bulb into the centre of the cross, pointy end up (that's where the shoot will emerge). If you're not sure which way is up, don't worry. Bulbs are clever and will find their own way to the surface. Press the soil back down gently with your foot and water well.

OCTOBER

WHAT YOU NEED

- Rotary scrubbing tool or bucket and sponge
- Vinegar
- Squeegee

TECHNIQUE
How to prepare your greenhouse for winter

As part of your overall prep for the end of the year, it's a good idea to give your greenhouse a good deep clean. A tidy, clear greenhouse doesn't just look better, it also prevents pests and diseases from overwintering and robbing you of a strong start in spring.

WHY DO THIS NOW
If you do this before winter sets in, your greenhouse will be pest- and disease-free when you want to use it in the spring. The glass is often far dirtier than it looks, and grime reduces the amount of light your plants receive. This is especially important if you're thinking about using your greenhouse over winter.

1
Clear the greenhouse completely. Remove any dead plants and sweep away dirt and moss.

2
Clean out staging, shelving, and guttering.

3
To clean the glass, mix equal parts warm water and vinegar for an effective homemade cleaner, or use a specialist greenhouse detergent. Wash both inside and out. If you have a rotary scrubbing tool then it can be used here. Otherwise you can clean the glass using a bucket and a sponge.

4
Rinse thoroughly, then use a squeegee to prevent streaks. Your greenhouse will be sparkling, pest-free, and ready to give your plants the best start next season.

WHAT YOU NEED

- Secateurs
- Breathable fleece
- String or twine
- Straw, leaves, or bracken

TROUBLESHOOTING
How to prepare tropical plants for winter

I love tropical plants — they bring so much drama to a garden. Lush leaves, bold colours, and that instant holiday feeling. But as soon as autumn edges in, it's time to think about how they'll survive the colder months. With a little care, plants like canna lilies, gingers, bananas, and even tree ferns can make it through winter, ready to explode into life again next year.

WHY DO THIS NOW
Protect your tropical plants now before the colder winter weather arrives so that they will survive into the following year.

DON'T LEAVE UNPROTECTED
Canna lilies cannot be left out over winter without protection.

BRING POTS INSIDE
Before the first frost, where possible move potted tropicals into a bright, sheltered spot. A conservatory, greenhouse, or south-facing window is perfect. If they're too big, a frost-free shed or garage will do. If you're able to do this, that's it, you're done! If you can't bring your plants inside, prep them for staying outdoors by cutting back and wrapping.

CUT BACK AND COVER
Some plants, like cannas, benefit from being cut back in the autumn. Cut them down to around 15cm (6in), and you can use the chopped foliage as a natural mulch or teepee over the root crown (the part of the plant just above the surface of the soil) for insulation.

WRAPPING TROPICAL PLANTS
Not all tropicals are treated the same. Tree ferns, for example, benefit from wrapping without being cut back. Tie the leaves loosely to the trunk with twine, cover the plant with straw or leaves, then wrap with breathable fleece to keep out cold and wet. Bananas need to be cut back first (**opposite**).

ADD INSULATION
Whether you have wrapped or cut back your plants, insulate them from the cold by piling straw, leaves, or bracken around the base. This keeps roots warm while still allowing air to circulate. Choose natural materials for this and avoid plastic, which traps moisture and causes rot. If you can, move your plants somewhere more sheltered like the side of the house to give them some respite from the worst of the winter winds.

144

OCTOBER

- **DECIDING WHAT TO DO**
- There's no simple way to know which method to use, you'll need to look up your plant's variety for information or ask at your local garden centre.

1

Cut off all the banana leaves just above the top of the main stem. Make the cut on a slight angle, sloping away from the centre, this helps stop moisture from sitting on the stem and causing rot.

2

Now wrap the trunk tightly but gently in layers of breathable fleece to keep it warm and protected from harsh winds and frost. For extra insulation, you can stuff a little straw under the fleece for very cold nights.

3

Don't forget the base. Cover it generously with mulch, compost, or straw to keep the roots snug and dry through winter's chill. Come spring, you can unwrap it and watch new shoots emerge strong and full of life, ready to bring that lush, tropical vibe back to your garden.

WHAT YOU NEED

- An old pallet or wood
- Saw
- Screws
- Drill
- Organic material (pinecones, bamboo canes, bark, and twigs)
- Wire netting
- Hammer
- Nails or staples
- Hook or hanging plate

PROJECT
How to make a bug hotel

You'll often see bug hotels for sale in garden centres, but honestly, they're one of the easiest (and most fun) things to make yourself. They give a home to all sorts of beneficial insects, including solitary bees, ladybirds, spiders, and more. In return, you get free pollination and natural, chemical-free pest control. They're also a great way to recycle bits of garden waste into something useful and educational.

WHY DO THIS NOW
Many insects are looking for places to shelter before winter so now is the perfect time to give them somewhere to stay.

1 Build a box about 15cm (6in) deep using leftover pallet wood, or whatever you have to hand. When you're making the structure, keep it simple. You can create your own design but here I've used two longer sections of wood with four shorter pieces to make the top, bottom and sections inside. Attach the pieces together with screws.

OCTOBER

2
Add a back to your box with screws. Then put one type of organic materials into each section so it's snug. You can also use some wire netting to hold in the contents. This can be attached with nails or staples.

SITING YOUR BUG BOX

Half the joy of a bug box is being able to watch the action, so put it somewhere you can see. It's amazing how fascinating those little bugs and bees are once you start paying attention. For most bugs it doesn't matter too much where you put the shelter, as long as it's not going to be disturbed. However, if you want to attract solitary bees, placement is important so bear the following in mind:
- **Face the sun** Bees love warmth, so south or south-east is perfect.
- **Height matters** Fix it at least 1m (3ft) off the ground.
- **Keep the entrance clear** Place it near vegetation if you like, but don't let plants block the holes.
- **Keep it steady** Make sure it's firmly fixed and won't wobble in the wind.

3
Attach a hook or metal plate with holes in so you can hang your bug hotel or you can just place it on the ground.

WHAT YOU NEED

- Bulbs
- Vase or pot
- Compost
- Decorative gravel (optional)

PROJECT
How to plant amaryllis bulbs for a Christmas display

I love amaryllis as part of a Christmas display. They're bold, beautiful, and easy to grow, as long as you give them the right start. You'll need an amaryllis bulb, a pot that's slightly wider than the bulb, and some compost. A vase works too, but be careful not to over-water, as amaryllis don't like sitting in soggy soil.

WHY DO THIS NOW
Planting the bulbs at the end of October will give you flowers by Christmas — they take around 6–8 weeks from planting to bloom.

1
Part-fill your container with compost.

2
Place the bulb pointy end up in the compost so only half to two-thirds of it is covered.

OCTOBER

3
Backfill around the bulb, then water once to saturate the soil. Don't water again until you see a flower bud emerge. If you like, add some decorative gravel on top.

4
Leave in a cool, dry place and in 6–8 weeks you'll have a stunning display just in time for Christmas.

WHAT YOU NEED

- Auger, bulb planter, or trowel
- Bulbs
- Watering can or hosepipe

TECHNIQUE
How to plant spring bulbs in a border

Planting bulbs can feel like a chore, but with a few simple tricks you can get the job done quickly and efficiently. You can do this by hand, but as the soil becomes harder towards winter, I like to keep things low effort and use a bulb auger. You can also use an auger bit in an electric drill to make the job easier.

WHY DO THIS NOW
Bulbs need time to grow their roots and a colder period of weather, to trigger flowering in the spring. You can plant bulbs from September to November although it's best to wait until the end of October to plant tulip bulbs.

1
Dig a hole three times the height of the bulb and about the same width. The holes should be at least twice a bulb's own width apart. To make the hole you can use an auger (**left**), a bulb planter (**below**), or a trowel.

NOVEMBER

2
Place each bulb in a hole with its nose pointing upwards.

3
Once positioned, cover the bulbs with the excavated soil, gently firming it down with your hands to remove air pockets. Avoid pressing too hard or walking over the area, as compacted soil can crush the bulbs and hinder root growth. Finally, water lightly to help the soil settle.

WHAT YOU NEED

- Hosepipe
- Hose reel (optional)

TECHNIQUE
How to prepare your garden hose for winter

Cold weather and leftover water in a confined space is a recipe for disaster, so if you want your garden hose to survive the winter in one piece, a little prep now will save you from a split, cracked mess come spring.

WHY DO THIS NOW
Taking these simple steps to look after your hose will ensure it doesn't incur damage over winter and is in good shape for when you next want to use it.

1
Disconnect the hose and, if possible, isolate the outside tap from the mains. If you've not already done so, insulate the tap (see p.154).

2
Drain any water from the spray nozzle of your hose and remove it. Also take off any non-return valves or connectors so they don't hold water that could freeze.

152

NOVEMBER

3
Empty the hose itself. Lay one end flat on the ground and slowly raise the rest of the hose so water runs out. If water sits inside during a freeze, it can expand and split the hose.

4
Coil the hose for storage. If you have a reel, use it; if not, make large, gentle loops so there are no tight kinks left in place over winter. Store the hose indoors if you can, in a shed, garage, or even inside the house. A dry, frost-free space will keep it in top condition until next year.

WHAT YOU NEED

- Insulating cap
- Foam lagging
- Tape or cable ties

TECHNIQUE
How to insulate outdoor taps

Leaving your garden tap exposed over the winter can cause serious trouble. Water left in pipes freezes, expands, and can crack the plumbing, turning a simple tap into a very expensive headache.

WHY DO THIS NOW
A little preparation now keeps everything in working order for next spring.

1
Start indoors at the isolation valve (usually under a sink) and turn it off. Then head outside and turn on the tap so any remaining water can drain away.

2
Remove hoses, sprinklers, and any other fittings. Even a tiny bit of trapped water can freeze and damage your pipework.

3
Cover the tap with a purpose-made insulating cap. These usually have a polystyrene core and a tough outer shell to block the cold. For any exposed pipes, wrap them with foam lagging and secure with tape or cable ties.

4
Check that the cap and any other cover is sitting firmly and won't blow away in the wind.

NOVEMBER

WHAT YOU NEED
- Rake
- Lawnmower

TECHNIQUE
How to do the last mow of the year

People often ask me, "When do I put the mower away for winter?" The truth is that grass doesn't suddenly stop growing because the temperatures dip, it just slows down, so there is no hard-and-fast rule about exactly when to mow your lawn for the last time before winter. Follow the tips below to make your decision.

WHY DO THIS NOW
If you do this at the right time your lawn can head into winter strong, and you'll get a greener, healthier bounce-back when spring rolls around.

TIDY UP
Clear away leaves, twigs, and any other debris with a rake before winter sets in. A blanket of soggy leaves might look seasonal, but on your lawn it's bad news, blocking light and air, and giving disease an open invitation.

BEAT THE FROST
Keep an eye on your lawn. If it's still growing, it still needs cutting. For most gardens, that means mowing right up until late autumn, sometimes even into November. Aim to give it a final tidy-up about a week before the first frost is due.

CHECK THE LENGTH
Leave grass too long and it flops over under frost, rain, or snow, creating damp, matted patches where fungi thrive. That's how problems like snow mould creep in. Shorter grass, meanwhile, stays upright, resists damage, and recovers more quickly in spring.

LOVE YOUR MOWER
Before you put your mower away for the winter show it some love, wiping away grass clippings and oiling the blades. Store it in a shed or garage out of the elements. If it has a battery, remove it and bring it indoors.

WHAT YOU NEED

- Old pair of tights
- Scissors

TECHNIQUE
How to keep your pots tidy with an old pair of tights

I'm always having to chase old pots around the garden. The slightest breeze and they scatter from my neat "pile" in the corner. This hack is perfect for keeping them in one place, ready for potting on cuttings or transplanting plants.

WHY DO THIS NOW
November is a great time to make the garden tidy and prepare everything for the following year and you won't need to hunt around looking for a pot next time you need one.

1
Take an old pair of tights. If they have a hole at the end of the foot, tie a knot in them to make a solid base. You can use the tights as they are or tear them in half and just use one leg.

2
Stack your pots inside, pushing them down to the toe.

NOVEMBER

3
Add as many pots as you can fit, then hold the tights fabric together at the top so it's ready to hang up.

DIFFERENT SIZES
You could have a few of these hanging up with different-sized pots in each one so that you can access what you need more easily.

4
Hang the whole thing up somewhere out of the way, and when you need a pot, just snip open the toe, pull one out, and then knot it back up again.

WHAT YOU NEED

- Watering can
- Pot feet
- Plant caddy (optional)
- Insulating material

TROUBLESHOOTING
How to protect pots from frost

Frost isn't just a problem for plants; it can also damage the pots themselves. When soil freezes, it expands, putting pressure on roots and on the container. Terracotta and some ceramics are especially vulnerable, and once they split, there's no fixing them. A few simple steps can save you the heartbreak, and the expense, of losing both pot and plant.

WHY DO THIS NOW
Take action now and your pots will be safe from winter frosts later.

BEFORE A FROST

WATER PLANTS
Giving your plants a water before a frost helps protect them because moist soil holds heat better than dry soil. Watering them the day before a cold snap will help insulate their roots. Don't let them sit soggy, though, just a thorough watering is enough.

PLACE ON A STAND
Perch pots on pot feet, bits of wood, or even a couple of old bricks. Pots sitting directly on cold, wet ground are more likely to freeze and crack. Not only does this protect against frost, but it also improves drainage as your plants aren't sitting in icy cold water.

NOVEMBER

DURING A FROST

MOVE POTS
If you can, move containers into a frost-free spot; a greenhouse, cold frame, unheated garage, shed, or even a porch. They don't need to be warm, just out of direct frost. Use a plant caddy to move heavier pots if you have one — or ask a friend to help!

GROUP POTS TOGETHER
For pots that are too heavy to move, try clustering them against a house wall or under an overhang. Walls radiate a little warmth, and grouping plants close together creates a mini "microclimate" where they protect each other from the cold.

ADD INSULATION
If pots can't be shifted, insulate them where they stand. Bubble wrap, horticultural fleece, hessian, or even an old blanket will do the trick. You're essentially keeping the frost from reaching the roots too quickly. Just make sure to leave the top of the plant uncovered so it can still breathe and have access to light.

WHAT YOU NEED

- Secateurs
- Spade or fork
- Gloves (optional)
- Compost
- Pot
- Mulch

TECHNIQUE
How to prepare borderline hardy plants for winter

How you protect your plants for winter depends on the species or variety and where you live. Some are happy with a thick mulch at the base, while others need insulation (see pp.158–159). Container-grown plants might need to be moved somewhere sheltered or frost-free, while tubers and rhizomes (think dahlias and cannas) can be lifted and stored until spring. Check with your local garden centre if you're unsure about a particular plant.

WHY DO THIS NOW
It's best to be prepared for the colder months and protect plants that need it now. For plants that need lifting, late autumn before the ground freezes is the best time. If you're mulching get to work before the heavy frosts.

STORING TUBERS
Lift your tubers, and hang them upside down to dry before storing.

LIFTING PLANTS

When foliage starts to die back on tubers or rhizomes, it's time to lift and move them somewhere sheltered for winter.

1
Snip stems down to a few centimetres above the base with secateurs.

2
Gently dig around the clump, taking care not to jab the tubers or rhizomes as they damage easily. Shake off as much soil as you can.

3
Leave them somewhere airy to dry for a few days.

4
Put them into a box or pot and cover them with dry compost. Make sure it's really dry to avoid them rotting. Place them somewhere frost-free until spring.

NOVEMBER

MULCHING PLANTS IN BORDERS

For plants that stay in the ground, timing is crucial. Protect frost-sensitive varieties before the cold sets in, while those that tolerate a light frost can wait a little longer.

1
Use organic materials like bark chippings, straw, leaf mould, or even the plant's own fallen leaves.

2
Spread a thick layer (around 5cm/2in) around the base, focussing on the crown.

3
Check the mulch occasionally through winter and top it up if it settles.

- **DECIDING WHAT TO DO**
- Not every plant needs winter protection. Check their hardiness rating and your garden's conditions to decide what action is best to take.

PLANTS THAT MAY NEED PROTECTION

Depending where you live plants that may need mulching or protecting include penstemon, evergreen agapanthus, some salvias, and fuschias. Plants that may need lifting include dahlias, gladiolus, cannas, and begonias.

PLANTS TO MULCH

AGAPANTHUS

PENSTEMON

SALVIA

PLANTS TO LIFT

DAHLIA

GLADIOLUS

BEGONIA

WHAT YOU NEED

- Wire brush
- Screwdriver
- White vinegar
- Salt
- Glass
- Surgical spirit or disinfectant wipe
- Tool sharpener
- Cloth
- Linseed oil
- Machine oil
- Bucket
- Sand

TECHNIQUE
How to prepare your garden tools for winter

Your tools are essential for your garden; they dig, chop, prune, weed, and transplant so we don't have to do it all by hand. But, like anything, they will wear out if you don't give them a bit of care. A little off-season care means your spades, secateurs, and forks can last for years without you having to splash out on replacements.

WHY DO THIS NOW
With just an afternoon of care, your tools will be sharper, safer, and ready to go when the new gardening season rolls around.

1
Knock off loose mud, then scrub away anything stubborn with water and a wire brush. If you've got caked-on clumps, gently scrape with a screwdriver. Dry the tools properly afterwards.

2
Pop rusty tools in a glass of white vinegar mixed with a handful of salt and leave them to soak for a couple of hours. The acidity will eat away at surface rust. After soaking, scrub with a wire brush or scourer.

NOVEMBER

3
Wipe down blades with surgical spirit or a disinfectant wipe. This kills off lingering fungi or bacteria that could spread between plants next season. Give all blades a quick sharpen with a whetstone or diamond sharpener. Blunt tools are more dangerous (and frustrating) than sharp ones.

4
Once clean, use a cloth to rub in a layer of linseed oil to prevent rust. For moving parts like hinges, a drop of machine oil will keep everything smooth.

5
Store your tools in a dry place. An airy shed or garage is ideal. For small hand tools, try storing them blade-down in a bucket of sand mixed with a splash of linseed oil. The sand cleans and the oil protects. Bigger tools like spades and forks are best hung up or stored upside down so their edges don't dull.

WHAT YOU NEED

- Decorative gravel or compost
- Vase or container
- Paperwhite bulbs

PROJECT
How to plant paperwhites for a Christmas display

These elegant, fragrant flowers are a type of narcissus that are quick and easy to grow, and they look stunning as a festive centrepiece. One note of warning — some people are not partial to the smell of these flowers, so avoid displaying them in small, confined spaces if that's you! There are lots of planting options here — you can use a dish or vase, some compost, gravel, or horticultural grit. A tall vase works well as it helps support the stems as the plants grow.

WHY DO THIS NOW
Planting narcissus paperwhites by mid-November means that they'll bloom in time for Christmas.

1
Add at least 2.5cm (1in) of gravel or compost to the bottom of your container. If you use gravel you can easily see the water level.

2
Place the bulbs with the pointy end facing upwards, pushing them into the growing medium. They can be planted close together, even touching each other.

NOVEMBER

- **PLANTING TIMES**
- Paperwhites bloom about 4–6 weeks after planting so you can plant them to flower when suits you, or plant several pots in succession so you have flowers from Christmas to New Year.

3
Add water until it reaches the base of the bulbs, but never submerge them. If using gravel, the top of the layer is a good guide. If you're planting in soil, check the moisture by touch and water when it begins to dry.

Water level to the base of the bulbs

4
Keep the container indoors in a sunny position, and by Christmas Day you'll have a beautiful display of blooms, perfect for bringing a little winter cheer.

WHAT YOU NEED

- Net
- Secateurs
- Pond heater, floating de-icer or saucepan

TECHNIQUE
How to care for ponds over winter

A pond can be the jewel of a garden. It draws the eye, brings sound and movement, and quietly supports a surprising amount of wildlife, from frogs and newts to thirsty birds and insects.

WHY DO THIS NOW

During the summer, ponds are fairly self-sustaining, ticking along with little intervention apart from the odd bit of weeding or trimming. Come autumn and winter though, your pond will appreciate a little extra care to keep it healthy.

1
Clear out leaves and debris as they release nutrients that encourage algae and pollute the water. A simple fix is to stretch a fine mesh net across the pond before too many leaves fall. You can also scoop out leaves every few days with a net to keep the water clear.

2
Prune hardy plants before the cold sets in — snip back dying stems and remove any yellowing foliage. Bring tender or tropical plants (water hyacinths or certain lilies) indoors. A conservatory, greenhouse, or even a bright windowsill will keep them ticking over until the frosts have passed. A sunny indoor pond tub or container with shallow water works well, and remember to change the water to stop it going stagnant before reintroducing in spring.

NOVEMBER

3
Care for your fish – they slow down as water temperatures drop. Their metabolism becomes sluggish, and they can no longer digest food properly. Gradually reduce feeding as autumn progresses and stop altogether once the water is consistently cold (below around 10°C/50°F).

4
Stop the pond freezing solid as it can spell disaster for pond life. A pond heater or floating de-icer (right) helps keep a patch of water open. Alternatively, hold a saucepan of hot (not boiling) water on the ice until it melts through. Never smash the ice with a hammer or stick – it sends shockwaves through the water that can harm or even kill fish. Topping up the water every so often is also a good habit.

5
Remove and clean pumps and filters, and store them somewhere dry and frost-free, like a shed or garage. Leaving them in the pond risks freezing damage and can shorten their lifespan. Fountains and waterfalls are best switched off too as running water in sub-zero weather can cause trouble. Pipes can freeze, equipment can crack, and moving water can empty parts of the pond.

WHAT YOU NEED

- Hori hori knife or trowel
- Mulch
- Rake

TECHNIQUE
How to mulch

If there was one thing I wish people would do in their gardens more, it probably would be to mulch. There are so many benefits to it, and it really sets your garden up for an easier year with less maintenance. Mulch is used on the top layer of the soil to control weeds, retain moisture, regulate temperature, and even improve the soil structure. It really does so much and there's loads of different types, but they're all applied in the same way.

WHY DO THIS NOW
Mulching is best done in the spring or autumn for trees, shrubs, roses, and perennials to give your plants the best conditions over the growing season to come.

1
Prepare the ground by removing any weeds with a hori hori knife or trowel. Don't skip this first stage — while mulch will suppress weeds, it won't help to start with them already in the soil.

MULCH TYPES
Each type of mulch has its trade-offs. Bark chips last well but take ages to break down. Compost feeds the soil but needs topping up often. Gravel is low-maintenance but doesn't add nutrients. Leaf mould is great for wildlife and keeping moisture in, though it breaks down quickly. Choose your mulch based on your priorities for your garden.

NOVEMBER

2
Add a layer of your chosen mulch 5cm (2in) thick onto the bed or around key plants. Bear in mind that a really thick layer of mulch will suppress more weeds, but bulbs and other plants will also find it hard to grow through.

3
Use a rake or your hands to make sure the mulch is evenly distributed. You don't want any high or low points, make sure it's even.

4
Make a little room around the base of plants, trees, and shrubs so that they're not in direct contact with the mulch. If the mulch is touching the stems of any existing plants, you run the risk of fungal diseases and stem rot.

169

WINTER

The quiet season, winter, is a time for rest, both for you and your plants. The relentless pace spurred on by new growth slows right down, but there are still a few useful jobs to tackle. You'll mainly be in maintenance phase now, but there are still a few planting jobs to be done. If it's too cold outside but you're itching to garden, there are also plenty of indoor projects you can do to brighten up your home too.

DECEMBER

- **172** How to keep poinsettia alive
- **174** How to pick the best fresh Christmas tree
- **176** How to keep your cut Christmas tree looking fresh longer
- **178** How to make fat balls for birds
- **180** How to winter wash trees
- **182** How to sprout mung beans in a jar

JANUARY

- **184** How to repurpose your Christmas tree
- **186** How to winter prune wisteria
- **188** How to winter prune deciduous ornamental trees
- **190** How to winter prune apple and pear trees
- **192** How to plant bare-root plants
- **194** How to grow microgreens
- **196** How to make soil blocks
- **198** How to sow summer bedding plants from seed

FEBRUARY

- **200** How to winter prune roses
- **202** How to prune a climbing rose
- **204** How to propagate roses from hardwood cuttings
- **206** How to manage ornamental grasses
- **207** How to prune citrus trees
- **208** How to make your own biodegradable pots
- **210** How to grow sweet peas from seed
- **212** How to add immediate colour

WHAT YOU NEED

- Watering can

TECHNIQUE
How to keep poinsettia alive

If your poinsettia never makes it past Christmas, you're not alone. They're tropical plants and so can struggle in cooler climates, but with a little care, you can keep them thriving well into the new year.

WHY DO THIS NOW
Looking after your poinsettia in the weeks just before or after Christmas when your plant is healthy and strong will extend its lifespan into the new year.

WHAT TO LOOK FOR
Start with a healthy plant. Look for dark green leaves right down to the soil and perky red bracts (those "petals" are actually leaves). Leave behind anything that's been parked by a draughty shop door or left outside, cold air will have nipped it already and it won't last long.

DECEMBER

DIFFERENT VARIETIES
Poinsettias are famous for their classic red bracts, but they come in many colours beyond that festive favourite. You can find varieties in white, pink, peach, burgundy, and even marbled or speckled mixes of red and cream.

HOW TO GET IT HOME
Once you've picked your plant, protect its leaves for the journey home and never leave it in the car overnight.

LOOKING AFTER IT
At home, find a bright spot away from radiators, fireplaces, and draughts; somewhere with plenty of daylight and no sudden chills. Check the compost before you water. If the top feels dry, give it a drink, but don't let it sit in a puddle. Soggy roots are the quickest route to a sad, leafless stick.

WHAT YOU NEED

- Measuring tape

TECHNIQUE
How to pick the best fresh Christmas tree

If you've ever stood in a Christmas tree lot wondering whether to go for a Nordmann or a Fraser fir, you're not alone. There are many excellent choices when it comes to Christmas tree types, each with their own strengths. Look for a sustainable local grower, where possible.

WHY DO THIS NOW
If you make the right choice for your home and situation your Christmas tree will look its best for as long as possible.

TIPS FOR PICKING THE BEST CUT CHRISTMAS TREE

- **Get to know the different types** Christmas trees vary in size, shape, scent, and some drop needles while others don't. The panel opposite can help you decide what type of tree will suit you.

- **Consider the size** Have a look at the size and shape of the tree to ensure that it will fit into your space and don't forget to include the stand and the decoration on the top in your calculation. You could measure the tree to make sure it will fit. Pick the one that works for your space and lifestyle, and you can't go wrong.

- **Spot the signs of a healthy tree** Check how fresh the tree is by pulling on a branch and seeing whether the needles stay attached. Make sure they're green and fresh, not brown and hard.

DECEMBER

COMMON TYPES OF CHRISTMAS TREE

NORWAY SPRUCE
A traditional favourite, the Norway spruce has a classic pyramid shape and lovely scent. However, this one needs a lot of water to prevent needle droppage, so it's not great in high traffic areas or homes with pets or very young children.

NORDMANN FIR
A tall, stately, non-drop classic, the Nordmann fir is child- and pet-friendly. While it has little or no scent, its wide base is perfect if you have a larger space to fill.

BLUE SPRUCE
With striking bluish-grey needles the blue spruce has a beautifully symmetrical form. The needles are quite sharp, so gloves are a good idea when handling. It holds its needles better than the Norway spruce, which is a bonus.

THE FRASER FIR
A popular option, the Fraser fir has a slender, elegant shape that's ideal for smaller rooms. It has a gorgeous citrus scent, holds its needles well, and, like the Nordmann, is safe for children and pets.

SHOULD YOU GET A POT-GROWN CHRISTMAS TREE?

If you want a Christmas tree that's beautiful, sustainable, and keeps on giving, a pot-grown tree is hard to beat. Plus, if you look after it properly, it'll bring you joy year after year.

Here are three reasons why a pot-grown tree makes the perfect choice.

- **Unlike cut or potted trees,** pot-grown Christmas trees have intact root systems, making them healthier, stronger, and far more likely to survive after the festive season.

- **They're sustainable and cost-effective,** and you can keep them year after year, either in their pot or planted outside, saving money and reducing waste.

- **They are versatile;** they look great outdoors all year round, but can also be brought indoors for Christmas, whether that's as the main tree, a kitchen tree, or even a bedroom tree. Just be sure to acclimatize them before putting them back outside again.

WHAT YOU NEED

- Handsaw
- Tree stand
- Jug or watering can
- LED lights

TECHNIQUE
How to keep your cut Christmas tree looking fresh longer

Now you've selected your tree, how do you help it to last through the full festive season? We all know to keep a cut Christmas tree watered, but a few extra steps can make it look fresher for longer.

WHY DO THIS NOW

Taking care of your tree as soon as you buy it will keep it looking good throughout the holiday season.

1
Before placing your tree in the stand, make a fresh cut across the base. This removes any hardened sap so the tree can absorb more water and stay greener for longer.

DECEMBER

2
Pick the right spot. Keep your tree away from direct sunlight, radiators, and fireplaces, as heat will dry it out quickly. You could lower the room temperature to help it last longer. Once you're happy with its position add plenty of water to the pot or stand then remove the netting.

- **WATERING YOUR TREE**
- When you bring a cut Christmas tree home, keep the base constantly hydrated. Start by filling the stand with at least 1 litre (1¾ pints) of water (or enough to cover the freshly cut base) and check it daily. Trees can drink a surprising amount, especially in the first week. Refill as needed, making sure the water never drops below the cut.

3
Use LED lights. Most people have these now, but if you haven't made the switch yet, they give off very little heat, which helps prevent the needles from drying out and reduces the risk of fire, while still keeping your tree beautifully lit.

WHAT YOU NEED

- Mixing bowl
- Any bird-friendly dry ingredients, such as oats, bread or cake crumbs, grated cheese, currants, raisins, sultanas, unsalted peanuts, grated apple or pear, or mealworms
- Lard or beef suet
- Small saucepan
- Spoon
- Old yoghurt pots (or coconut shells)
- String or twine

PROJECT
How to make fat balls for birds

When frosts bite and worms vanish, the birds in your garden need a little extra something to help them stay plump and warm. Fat balls are just the ticket. Sure, you can grab them at the shops, but making your own is dead simple, fun, and often cheaper. It's a great way to repurpose leftover bits from your kitchen, too.

WHY DO THIS NOW
This is the time of year when the temperature drops and garden birds need our help to stay warm and fed.

1
Put all the dry ingredients into the bowl. Stick to roughly one part fat to two parts dry mix – that keeps everything solid and easy to shape. Gently melt the lard or suet in the saucepan. Once melted, pour the fat over the dry mix and stir until everything becomes glossy and holds together.

2
Poke a hole through the bottom of a yoghurt pot. Thread the string through and secure it with a knot or loop. Repeat with other pots if you have more mixture to use.

DECEMBER

3
Fill the pot with your sticky birdy mixture, pressing down firmly. Ensure the knot is at the top of the mixture so it doesn't fall off your string when you remove the pot. Pop it into the fridge and leave to firm up overnight.

WHAT TO AVOID
- **Turkey fat** doesn't firm up properly and can leave birds' feathers matted, which is not good for flying.
- **Raisins or sultanas** are toxic to canines, so skip them if you've got a dog.
- **Only use mealworms** if no hedgehogs visit your garden as they can be harmful to them.

4
Slice through the pot, peel it away, and you've got a solid fat ball dangling and ready to hang up.

WHAT YOU NEED

- Oil and water solution
- Sprayer

TECHNIQUE
How to winter wash trees

Winter washing your fruit trees helps to control the eggs, larvae, and nymphs of pests like green fly, black fly, and woolly aphids, as well as diseases. While most commonly done for fruit trees, this can also be done for other deciduous trees and shrubs, if needed. It kills overwintering eggs, removes debris, and reduces fungal spores. The process involves spraying the bark with a mixture of plant oils and water — you'll find the concentrate in your local garden centre.

WHY DO THIS NOW
Doing this when there is no foliage makes it easier to spray the trunks and branches and means that your tree will be ready for new growth in the spring.

1
Mix the solution following the supplier's guidance and apply to a sprayer. Check the chamber at the top of the container so you know you're measuring the correct amount.

TYPES OF SPRAYER
Hand-pump sprayers are cheap, light, and perfect for a few plants or small gardens, but you've got to keep pumping. Electric sprayers do the hard work for you, covering bigger areas quickly and easily, great if you've got a larger garden or need to spray often.

DECEMBER

PROS AND CONS
Winter washing is especially useful for fruit trees like apple, cherry, and plum if they are producing less fruit and there are clear signs of pest damage. However, it can disturb or remove beneficial insects and hibernating wildlife, such as overwintering aphid predators and queen wasps, so consider this trade-off.

3
Cover the whole tree, getting into all the bark crevices, around the buds and the back. If you cover nearby plants and fences, rinse off with water.

2
Spray the solution on a dry, still day to prevent it being carried elsewhere by the wind. A powered backpack is quicker and easier than a hand spray but either way works.

WHAT YOU NEED

- Mung beans
- Glass jar
- Cheesecloth or kitchen paper
- Elastic band or tie

PROJECT
How to sprout mung beans in a jar

Want to grow a fresh, high-protein food in just a few days? Why not try sprouting mung beans? All you need is a jar and something to cover it with, and they provide a super quick crop. These are perfect for adding a nutritional boost to salads, stir-fries, and sandwiches.

WHEN TO DO THIS
Any time during the winter months. When the garden is quieter, there's time to try things that can happily grow indoors.

1
Add a small handful of mung beans to a jar. You don't need many, as they'll expand a lot.

2
Cover them with water, secure cheesecloth or kitchen paper over the top, and leave them overnight in a dark place to soak.

DECEMBER

3
The next day, drain the water completely.

4
Rinse the beans twice a day, each time draining well, and keep the jar in the dark.

5
In just a few days, you'll have a jar full of crunchy mung bean sprouts ready to harvest.

WHAT YOU NEED

- Secateurs
- Wood shredder
- Twine
- Saw
- Drill

PROJECT
How to repurpose your Christmas tree

After Christmas don't just chuck your tree on the pavement! There are plenty of ways to give it a second life.

WHY DO THIS NOW
Making use of your tree after Christmas when it's still fairly fresh and usable is a more sustainable choice than throwing it away.

USE THE BRANCHES

PROTECT BEDS AND CONTAINERS
Cut off the branches (**above**) and lay them over garden beds or containers to protect plants from frost (**right**).

MAKE FREE WOOD MULCH
If you have access to a shredder you can make wood mulch to use on your beds.

JANUARY

USE THE TRUNK

MAKE A TRELLIS
Make a trellis by planting the bare stump in the ground – perfect for climbing plants like sweet peas to use in the spring.

TURN THE TRUNK INTO A BUG HOTEL
Drill holes in each section to a depth of about 15cm (6in) (**above left**), then cut up the stump (**above right**). Stack them up (**above**) to create a cosy refuge for beneficial insects and other wildlife.

WHAT YOU NEED

- Twine
- Scissors
- Ladder
- Secateurs

TECHNIQUE
How to winter prune wisteria

Lots of people ask me why their wisteria isn't flowering in late spring and summer. This can happen if it's a young plant, it doesn't get enough sun, or it can be because it hasn't been pruned properly. If the age of the plant and lack of sunlight are not the issue, then the winter prune can often kick-start or improve flowering.

WHY DO THIS NOW

Pruning in winter as well as summer (see pp.78–79) will encourage the development of short spurs that carry the flowers in spring. If you don't prune in this way, you may end up with just leafy growth. Winter pruning is done in the dormant season, so January is the perfect month to get cracking.

1
Tie down some of the long, whippy growth to your support structure. It's important to do this before you do anything else if you're still training your wisteria. Do this either by threading it in and out of trellis or tying it down. Then you can pull out some of the longer stems that will need cutting.

JANUARY

CHOOSING YOUR WISTERIA
Don't buy a wisteria unless you've seen it has the ability to flower. Spring's the best time to do this because you can see the flower buds forming. That way you'll know your plant will bloom, rather than waiting years to find out you've got a leafy, non-flowering dud.

3
Prune any dead sections completely back to the base. Your wisteria should go from a whippy mess to something a lot less cluttered that will be ready to flower in spring.

2
Cut each stem back to two buds above the base, whether you summer pruned or not (see pp.78–79). Notice how I'm pruning on an angle just above the bud.

WHAT YOU NEED

- Secateurs

TECHNIQUE
How to winter prune deciduous ornamental trees

Ornamental trees, such as acers, silver birches, cherry trees, and magnolias, are grown for their beauty rather than to produce fruit or timber. When pruning them the goal is simple: tidy the tree up, keep it healthy, and work with its natural shape. Always make your cuts just above a healthy bud so new growth heads in the right direction.

WHY DO THIS NOW
It's best to do this while the tree is dormant, so any time between November and March before the sap starts to rise is suitable.

1
Remove any dead or diseased parts and any branches that cross and rub.

Dead material

2
Clear the trunk by taking off any smaller shoots, leaving a clean stem about 0.9–1.2m (3–4ft tall). Thin out overcrowded growth so the main branches are evenly spaced and the tree has an open, balanced form.

JANUARY

THE BEST ORNAMENTAL TREES TO GROW

There are a variety of ornamental trees to choose from, many of them have beautiful foliage or flowers, and come in compact and patio-friendly sizes, so can fit even into a small space.

AMELANCHIER
In spring, Amelanchier (Juneberry) covers itself in frothy white blossom, then turns out juicy berries the birds can't resist. Come autumn, the leaves blaze orange and red before falling.

JAPANESE MAPLE
The delicate, hand-shaped leaves of the Japanese maple (*Acer palmatum*) shift through shades of green, orange, and crimson, glowing in autumn light. They're slow growing, elegant, and happy in pots or borders.

CRAB APPLE
Crab apples (*Malus* spp.) put on a show in every season. Spring brings clouds of blossom buzzing with bees, followed by tiny, jewel-like fruits that feed birds all winter. They're tough and full of charm.

SILVER BIRCH
Silver birches (*Betula pendula*) light up a garden with their pale, peeling bark and airy, delicate leaves. They sway gracefully in the wind, casting dappled shade, and turn golden in autumn.

COMMON ELDER
Common elder (*Sambucus nigra*) brings drama with its dark, lacy foliage and airy form. In spring, delicate pink flowers appear, followed by glossy black berries that birds love.

HAWTHORN
Hawthorn (*Crataegus* spp.) bursts into clouds of white or pink flowers in late spring, filling the air with a gentle scent. Come autumn, bright red berries attract birds, while its thorny branches add winter structure.

WHAT YOU NEED

- Secateurs

TECHNIQUE
How to winter prune apple and pear trees

When it comes to fruit trees, such as apples and pears, the timing of your pruning makes all the difference. If you skip both winter and summer pruning (see pp.112–113), the tree will quickly turn into a wild tangle of shoots, which might look vigorous but won't do much for your fruit crop.

WHY DO THIS NOW
A good winter prune wakes the tree up and encourages fresh growth in spring.

1
Start by snipping out anything dead, damaged, or diseased. If you see shoots sprouting from the base of the trunk, take those off too. They're called suckers, and they grow from a different rootstock.

INCREASING YIELDS
Apples and pears carry their fruit on spurs – thick, wobbly shoots that stick out from the branches. These are the ones you want to encourage. Long, thin shoots may look busy but won't give you any fruit. Removing the long, thin shoots will let sunlight in and improve airflow, giving spurs the best conditions to produce lots of fruit.

Spur

JANUARY

- **TREE TYPES AND SHAPES**
  Decide what shape of tree to prune: standard, espalier, or cordon. For standard trees, aim for an open goblet shape (the classic tree shape) if you're growing standard trees. This lets in light and allows air to move around freely. If you're espalier or cordon training, follow those shapes instead.

2
Remove any branches that cross or rub against each other or compete for space. Where two or more stems sprout from the same spot, keep the strongest one and prune the rest.

3
Find last year's smooth new shoots (**above**) and cut them back by about a quarter to a third, just above a bud that's facing outwards, so it grows in the right direction (**right**). If the tree is getting tall or tangled, shorten bigger branches by up to a third. Cut back to the strongest outward or upward-facing branches to give your tree a balanced shape.

191

WHAT YOU NEED

- Bucket
- Spade
- Compost or manure
- Mycorrhizal fungi
- Cane or tape measure

TECHNIQUE
How to plant bare-root plants

Bare-root plants are sold in a dormant state without any soil around their roots and can be cheaper to buy as you don't have to pay for the soil or a pot. This also makes them lighter to move and plant. The roots are kept wrapped so they're moist until you put the plant in the soil. While it's not quite as simple to plant bare-root plants as it is potted ones, the results and money saved will be worth it.

WHY DO THIS NOW
Bare-root plants are sold between October and March when plants are dormant, giving the roots time to establish in a new location during the winter. This leads to quicker growth and reduced transplant shock compared to pot-bought plants. It also makes them easier and cheaper to dig up, transport, and plant.

1
Rehydrate your bare-root plant in a bucket of water for a minimum of two hours prior to planting.

2
Dig a hole that is wide and deep enough for the roots to spread out naturally, rather than being bent or crowded. Break up the soil at the base with a fork and add a spadeful of compost or well-rotted manure.

JANUARY

WHY PLANT A ROSE MORE DEEPLY?

To grow roses, they are grafted onto a rootstock, creating what's known as the graft union on the stem. Burying this keeps it protected from frosts, sun, and drying out, and helps the roots get established, leading to stronger, healthier growth.

3

Remove the plant from the bucket of water. If you want the plant to settle in faster you can hold it over the planting hole and sprinkle some mycorrhizal fungi on it, which will aid root development.

4

Place the plant in the hole at the original soil level on the stem. If this isn't obvious, position it so that the top of the root system sits just below ground level. A cane can help you measure this. If you're planting bare-root roses, the bottom of the stem should be 5cm (2in) below the top of the hole.

5

Backfill around the roots using the soil that was originally dug out to make the hole. Then lightly firm in the soil around your plant with your foot and give it plenty of water.

193

WHAT YOU NEED

- Old yoghurt pots or plastic trays
- Compost
- Leafy plant seeds
- Scissors

PROJECT
How to grow microgreens

If you fancy some homegrown produce during the winter months, microgreens — the tiny seedlings of herbs and salad plants — are a great place to start. They're packed with flavour, and quick to grow all year round on a sunny windowsill, in anything from seed trays to yoghurt pots. For a steady supply, sow a new batch each week so fresh leaves are always ready to snip and enjoy.

WHY DO THIS NOW

While you can do this at any time of year, it's great to have something fresh and homegrown to eat during the winter.

1
Grab a few containers. I like to use old takeaway tubs, but any small container will do. Fill them with a little compost, and firm in.

2
Empty full packets of leafy plant seeds into each container. Sow them thickly and don't worry about overcrowding.

JANUARY

- **WHICH SEEDS?**
- Use the seeds of plants
- you like the flavour of when
- they're fully grown. Here
- I'm using radish, pak choi,
- broccoli, and kale, but you
- can choose whatever you like.

3
Water lightly and stack the containers on top of each other. Weighing them down encourages optimal growth. Place an empty box on the top tray.

4
When they start to sprout (usually after just a couple of days), unstack them and place on a windowsill or somewhere bright. Start watering every one or two days to keep the compost moist.

5
After about a week, harvest the whole tray or just a few bits for a garnish by cutting off the growth with scissors. As long as you keep them watered, you can leave what you don't want immediately, and pick them when you're ready.

WHAT YOU NEED

- Pre-made or homemade soil blocking mix
- A soil blocker
- Watering can
- Tray or potting bench
- Seeds

PROJECT
How to make soil blocks

A soil block is a compressed cube of compost that holds together without a pot. As seedlings grow, their roots hit the edge, get "air-pruned", and branch out instead of circling round. This leads to stronger plants that establish quickly, suffer less transplant shock, and saves you from using plastic pots.

WHY DO THIS NOW
If you make soil blocks, you can get started now on planting your seeds for those plants that have a long growing season.

1
Buy or make some soil blocking mix. Make your own by combining one part topsoil, one part leaf mould, one part grit or vermiculite, and four parts coir compost.

2
Wet down the soil mix until it's wet, clumpy, and sticks together but is not too muddy. If the mixture is too dry, it will stick to the soil blocker and not come out cleanly. If too wet, your mix will simply fall out of the soil blocker. Combine your mix thoroughly.

JANUARY

3
Press the soil blocker into the potting mix. Pack it with even more dirt by pressing the soil blocker down into the potting mix again.

4
Release the blocks by pushing the blocker onto the bottom of a tray, pressing the handle, and gently pulling away the soil blocker.

5
Make a small hole and plant a seed inside the soil block, following the instructions for whatever seeding you're using. Fill the hole with a little potting mix or horticultural grit and water them from the bottom to keep the soil moist.

WHAT YOU NEED

- Seed propagator or seed tray with lid
- Compost
- Seeds of your choice

TECHNIQUE
How to sow summer bedding plants from seed

If you want instant impact in the garden, summer bedding is hard to beat — bright blocks of colour that just keep going for months. While garden centres are full of ready-grown plants in late spring, raising your own from seed is cheaper and gives you far more choice of varieties. Sow in January or February on a warm windowsill, in a greenhouse, or heated propagator with a lid. Seeds need steady warmth (of around 18–21°C/64–70°F) and good light to get started.

WHY DO THIS NOW
If you get going early in the year your seeds will be ready to plant out by spring — bedding plants take time to reach flowering stage.

1
Fill your seed tray, pots, or soil blocks (see pp.196–197) with seed compost, tap them down, and lightly firm the surface.

2
Scatter seeds evenly, then cover with a fine layer of compost.

JANUARY

3
Put the pots on the windowsill, greenhouse, or in your propagator. If in a propagator, open it every now and then to release condensation.

4
When seedlings appear, pick out the strongest and pot them on individually so they've got space to grow without competition.

SIX PLANTS TO GROW FROM SEED

Here is some inspiration for plants to grow yourself for hanging baskets, pots, and borders.

GERANIUM (PELARGONIUM)

BEGONIA

LOBELIA

ANTIRRHINUM (SNAPDRAGON)

SALVIA

SWEET PEA

WHAT YOU NEED

- Secateurs

TECHNIQUE
How to winter prune roses

A lot of people panic about pruning roses, worried they'll mess it up and kill the plant. However, roses are tough as nails and can handle a serious chop without fuss. It's really just a matter of knowing what type of rose you have and how much to take off.

WHY DO THIS NOW
Prune roses when they're dormant and with bare stems so it's easy to spot what needs cutting. It's also timed just before spring growth, so they bounce back quickly.

1
Cut out the brown or black dead wood (green wood is living).

— Living wood

— Dead wood

TYPES OF ROSES

- **Hybrid teas** These like a hard chop, down to about 10–15cm (4–6in) in height, so they grow back strong and upright.
- **Floribundas** Should be pruned to around 25–30cm (10–12in) in height to keep their bushy shape.
- **Shrub or patio roses** Lightly trim, taking about a third off, to keep them neat. If you don't know what type you have, cut down by up to half their height.
- **Climbing roses** Prune these in a slightly different way (see pp.202–203).

FEBRUARY

Remove crossing stems

2
Open up the centre of the plant by removing any crossing branches – these can rub, causing damage and inviting disease. You could use these cuttings for propagation (see pp.204–205).

45-degree angle

3
Remove weak growth. If a stem is thinner than a pencil, it's not worth keeping. It won't produce many flowers and will just make the plant look messy.

4
Trim the main canes. Reduce the overall height by one-third, cutting just above an outward-facing bud at a 45-degree angle (angled away from the bud). This encourages new growth in the right direction. Angle the cut to stop water sitting there, which encourages disease and rot.

WHAT YOU NEED

- Secateurs
- Twine or cable ties
- Scissors

TECHNIQUE
How to prune a climbing rose

Roses that climb or spread out come in two types, climbing roses and rambling roses, and they need to be pruned differently and at different times. Climbing roses are more upright and structured in growth and tend to have larger blooms, growing up against walls and fences.

WHY DO THIS NOW
Climbing roses are best pruned in February while they're dormant and leaf-free, making it easy to see the framework and tie in the strongest stems. Doing this just before spring growth also means the plant heals fast and puts energy into fresh shoots and plenty of flowers

Dead, brown wood, compared to the new growth next to it which is green

PRUNING RAMBLERS
Ramblers have smaller flowers and grow in a wilder style over arches and larger spaces. After flowering in late summer, remove any dead, diseased, or damaged stems right down to the base. Also cut out about a third of the oldest, thickest stems down to the base. Cut side shoots back to four healthy shoots. Select the new, flexible canes produced this year and tie them in. Avoid pruning the current year's growth as this will carry next year's flowers.

1
Remove dead, diseased, or dying branches. These will generally be black or brown and need to be cut off at the base. Also remove any weak stems completely (thinner than a pencil), as they won't hold a bloom in the summer.

FEBRUARY

Tie using twine or cable ties

2
Tie in any new shoots that need support. Tying the stems of your rose to its support structure helps it to climb and prevents the stems from breaking. Where possible, tie in the stems horizontally as this will encourage more flower-bearing side shoots to form.

3
Prune flowering side shoots back to two-thirds of their length on a 45-degree angle, just above the bud to stop water sitting on the cut, and to encourage growth in the right direction. You can use these to propagate new plants (see pp.204–205).

4
If the plant is heavily congested, then cut out any older branches (they may be grey, flaky, or have woody bark) from the base to promote new growth. Don't worry if the plant now looks sparse, it will soon grow back.

WHAT YOU NEED

- Tape measure
- Secateurs
- Pot
- 50:50 mix of compost and horticultural grit
- Watering can

TECHNIQUE
How to propagate roses from hardwood cuttings

Propagation is a fancy way to say you're growing new plants from seeds or taking cuttings. Buying a new rose may be easier, but there's no mystery to propagating them. Some take more quickly and easily than others, but at its core the process is pretty simple. Best of all? It's satisfying, budget-friendly, and helps you fill your garden for free.

WHY DO THIS NOW
Winter is also a good time to prune your roses (see pp.200–203), which, in turn, makes it a good time to propagate using the cuttings from prunings.

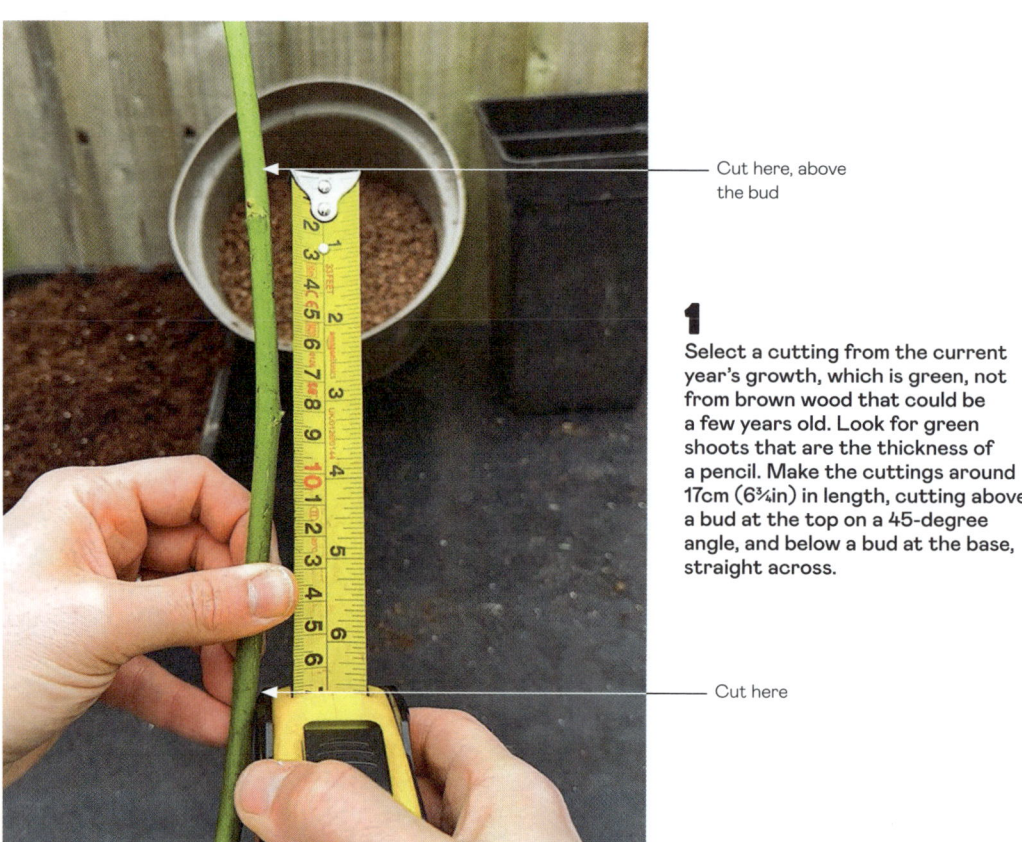

Cut here, above the bud

1
Select a cutting from the current year's growth, which is green, not from brown wood that could be a few years old. Look for green shoots that are the thickness of a pencil. Make the cuttings around 17cm (6¾in) in length, cutting above a bud at the top on a 45-degree angle, and below a bud at the base, straight across.

Cut here

FEBRUARY

2
Give the buds at the bottom of the cutting that will be in the soil a light scratch to promote rooting. The scratches should be light – don't cut into the plant too deeply.

Give the cutting a light scratch

3
If you're growing the roses in pots, insert several cuttings into the corners of a tall pot (one in each corner), with a 50:50 mix of compost and horticultural grit. Make sure at least two-thirds of the cuttings are covered. You can also put them straight in the ground if you prefer, following the same rules and keeping them 15cm (6in) apart.

4
Water them in, giving them a good soaking, then leave to root. This may take a few months; normally by the following summer they're ready to pot on into a bigger pot or plant out.

PLANT AROUND THE SIDE
Planting in the corners or the side of the pot reduces the chance of rot as water drains away faster there.

WHAT YOU NEED

- Secateurs
- Gloves

TECHNIQUE
How to manage ornamental grasses

Grasses come in two types — evergreen and deciduous. At this time of year, evergreen grasses will have some green from last year mixed in with the brown, while deciduous grasses are all brown from last season. To keep them looking their best, you need to prune them properly. Get it wrong and you can leave a messy cut line or even damage the plant.

WHY DO THIS NOW
If you prune your grasses now you can remove wet, decaying foliage that may damage the plant's new growth in the spring.

DECIDUOUS GRASSES
Prune deciduous grasses right down to the base unless you spot fresh green shoots, in which case cut just above those. Grasses don't grow from the top, so trimming into new growth will leave a permanent line.

EVERGREEN GRASSES
Take more care with evergreen grasses. You can use your hands to tease out the dead, brown bits, leaving the green intact. Gloves are a must here as ornamental grasses will shred your hands if you're not careful!

FEBRUARY

WHAT YOU NEED

- Secateurs

TECHNIQUE
How to prune citrus trees

Late winter is the best time to give your citrus trees a prune. While they don't typically need a lot of pruning, they can grow very large and leggy in pots, so regular pruning is a good idea.

WHY DO THIS NOW
During the winter months it's easier to see the structure of the tree so you can shape it properly. At this time of year while the tree is dormant, pruning causes less stress than it would during the growing season.

1
Prune out anything that's dead, diseased, or dying and then reshape the plant, always cutting just above a leaf node.

2
Prune back your plant by up to two-thirds to encourage bushy growth. The plant will start to bush out after this prune.

3
Cut back any crossing branches as these can chafe and create an access point for insects and disease. You can also remove the lower branches if you want to create a standard shape. Your citrus tree should now be a tight shape and can be put back outside once the weather warms up.

PROTECT FROM FROST
If your citrus tree is outside you'll need to cover it to protect it from the frost (see pp.158–159), so you may need to unwrap it before pruning in February.

WHAT YOU NEED

- Cardboard boxes
- Scissors or Stanley knife
- Bucket
- Glasses, jars, or cans
- Compost

PROJECT
How to make your own biodegradable pots

If you need pots for seeds or seedlings, want something sustainable, and don't like the idea of plastic pots, you can make your own biodegradable pots using just a cardboard box. These pots can be planted straight into the soil, leaving no waste and causing no transplant shock for your seedlings. Different materials break down at different rates, so you may wish to remove the plant from the pot before planting – either way this is an eco-friendly pot that can be recycled.

WHY DO THIS NOW

This is the perfect activity for this time of year when there's not so much to do in the garden and you have more time to get ready for sowing seeds and planting seedlings.

1
Remove any plastic tape or packaging from the cardboard.

2
Cut the cardboard into strips using scissors or a Stanley knife.

FEBRUARY

3
Soak the strips in a bucket of water for 10–15 minutes until they're soft and pliable.

4
Wrap the damp strips tightly around a jar, glass, or can, folding underneath so they overlap to create a secure base. Press down firmly to shape the bottom. Leave them to dry completely, then slide off the mould.

5
Fill your pots with compost and use them to plant seedlings.

WHAT YOU NEED

- Sweet pea seeds
- Root trainers or toilet rolls
- Compost
- Wigwam, trellis, obelisk, or bamboo canes

TECHNIQUE
How to grow sweet peas from seed

Whether you're after cottage garden vibes, love their scent, or want to have a go at growing something from seed, sweet peas are easy once you know how. Sow them between January and March. Sweet peas can also be sown in autumn and germinated in an unheated greenhouse or cold frame.

WHY DO THIS NOW
Starting your seeds early in the year gives them time to grow strong roots before you plant them out.

1
Soak the seeds overnight in water. Sweet pea seeds have tough coats so doing this softens them up and gets them germinating faster. This isn't essential, but it will give you a head start.

2
Give them space to stretch – sweet peas hate having their roots disturbed. Use root trainers (a type of deep pot) or cardboard tubes. Fill with compost and poke a seed about 1.5cm (½in) deep into each one.

FEBRUARY

3

Put them somewhere bright and cool once the seedlings appear (usually within 7–21 days) – a windowsill or gently heated greenhouse works fine. Keep the compost damp but not soggy. Remove the top growth once your seedlings have about 3–4 pairs of leaves. Pinch off between your finger and thumb just above a leaf joint to promote side shoot formation. It feels brutal, but encourages bushier plants and more flowers later on.

Pinch off just above a leaf joint

4

Move your plants outside when they look sturdy and the frosts are over. Harden them off by putting the plants out during the day and bringing them in at night for a week or so (see p.60). Then plant them out with ready-made supports or create a shape from bamboo canes to which their tendrils will cling.

211

WHAT YOU NEED

- Winter plants
- Compost
- Pots

PROJECT
How to add immediate colour

In late winter it can seem like forever until the vibrancy of spring arrives. So, if you need some flowers to brighten up these dull days, here are five that will give you immediate colour.

WHY DO THIS NOW
At this time of year, you may not have a lot of other colour in your garden so planting up some pots of bright flowers will lift the spirits.

WHAT TO CHOOSE
If you want cheerful winter pots, primulas, pansies, violas, dianthus, and bellis are brilliant. Plant taller primulas or dianthus in the middle or back, then layer pansies and violas around the edges for a carpet of colour. Sprinkle bellis in front for tiny pops of pink or white. Mix different colours for contrast, deep purples with bright yellows look amazing! They're hardy, so they'll survive frosty spells, and you can peek out of your window and enjoy blooms all winter. Keep the soil moist, and your pots will keep looking cheerful for months.

FEBRUARY

FIVE PLANTS TO ADD IMMEDIATE COLOUR IN WINTER

Here are my top plants to grow for early colour. They're all relatively easy to grow and look after and will bring instant joy.

PRIMULA
Easy to grow and coming in a variety of forms, primulas are versatile and suitable both for growing in borders and in containers.

BELLIS
A bedding daisy that has been bred from the original lawn weed, bellis is easy to grow and needs minimal fuss.

DIANTHUS
Dianthus has scented flowers that carry on into early summer. They will repeat flower if you keep deadheading them and they make great cut flowers too.

PANSIES AND VIOLAS
Need to know the difference at a glance? Pansies generally have larger blooms than violas. Both come in a wide range of colours, from white to almost black, and everything in between so you can choose a colour to suit your scheme.

POTTED SPRING BULBS
If you missed growing your own you can get a range of spring bulbs pre-potted. Also, if you're not ready to spend much time outside yet, they all look great indoors as well.

RESOURCES

VIDEOS
- **Instagram** @themichaelgriffiths
- **TikTok** @themichaelgriffiths
- **Facebook** @TheMichaelGriffiths
- **YouTube** @TheMichaelGriffiths

GENERAL GARDEN ADVICE
- **BBC Gardeners' World** gardenersworld.com
- **RHS** rhs.org.uk

FURTHER READING
- **For planting combinations:**
  What Grows Together by Jamie Butterworth
- **For garden design:**
  How to Design a Garden by Pollyanna Wilkinson

PLANT IDENTIFICATION APP
- **PictureThis**

NURSERIES
- **David Austin Roses** davidaustinroses.co.uk
- **Form Plants** formplants.com

GARDEN CENTRES
- **Dobbies** dobbies.com

TOOLS
- **Bulldog Tools** bulldogtools.co.uk
- **Kent & Stowe** kentandstowe.com
- **Ryobi** uk.ryobitools.eu

HOSES
- **Hozelock** hozelock.com

MULCH
- **Dalefoot Composts** dalefootcomposts.co.uk
- **Strulch** strulch.co.uk

SEEDS
- **Premier Seeds Direct** premierseedsdirect.com
- **She Grows Veg** shegrowsveg.com

WATER BUTT
- **The Dipping Tank Company**
  thedippingtankcompany.co.uk

LAWNCARE
- **Grass Gains** grassgains.co.uk

COMPOST WORMS
- **Wiggly Wigglers** wigglywigglers.co.uk

INDEX

A
acanthus 107
acer 188, 189
achillea 75
agapanthus 137, 161
Alchemilla mollis 107
allium 24, 132
amaryllis 148–9
Amelanchier (Juneberry) 189
antirrhinum 199
ants 39, 98–9
aphids 39
  see also blackfly; greenfly; woolly aphid
apple 112–13, 190
  see also crab apple
April 40–59
argyranthemum 85
aster 75, 135, 136
astilbe 54–5
August 108–21
autumn 122–69
azalea 85, 140

B
bacteria 163
banana 86, 87, 144
bare-root plants
  hedging 82–3
  planting 192–3
  strawberries 34–5
bark chips 168
basil 67, 95
BBQs, herbs for 94–5
bean sprouts 182–3
bedding plants 85, 198–9
beech 140
beer traps 57
bees 50, 147
  solitary 146
begonia 161, 199
bellis 212–13
biodegradable pots 208–9
biodiversity 50, 98

biological controls 57
birch, silver 188, 189
birds
  feeding 56, 127, 136–7, 178–9, 189
  nesting 64
black spot 69
blackfly 39, 180–1
blueberry 140
boiling water 31
bokashi composting 89
borderline hardy plants 87, 160–1
borders 54–5, 150–1
broccoli 195
brunnera 54–5, 107
buds 14, 15
bug hotels 146–7, 185
bulb augers 150–1
bulb vases 129
bulbs
  amaryllis 148–9
  deadheading 85
  hyacinth 128–9
  layering in pots 132–3
  planting in a border 150–1
  planting in lawns 142
  potted spring 132–3, 213
  protection for 133
  tidying 24
butterflies 50

C
calocephalus 134
camellia 85, 140
campanula 75
canna lily 86–7, 144, 160–1
centranthus 107
Chelsea chop 74–5
cherry 188
cherry laurel 64
Christmas
  and amaryllis 148–9
  and hyacinth 128–9
  and paperwhites 164–5
  and poinsettia 172–3

Christmas trees 174–7
  repurposing 184–5
chrysanthemum 135
citrus trees 207
clay 16–17
climbers
  deadheading 85
  hydrangea 80–1
  roses 200, 202–3
  tying in 70–1
clover lawns 50–1
coir 72, 196
cold frames 53, 60
coleus 67
colocasia 86
colour
  autumnal 134–5
  immediate 212–13
compaction, soil 41, 46–7
compost 168
  bokashi 89
  DIY 88–91
  and levelling lawns 124–5
  reusing last year's 116–17
  troubleshooting 91
compost bins 88–91, 98
conifers 135
container gardening
  and amaryllis 148–9
  and ants 99
  and autumn colour 134–5
  and biodegradable pots 208–9
  and Christmas 128–9, 164–5, 172–3, 175
  and feeding 92
  and frost protection 158–9
  and hanging baskets 72–3, 92
  and heatwaves 96
  and layering spring bulbs 132–3
  and microgreens 194–5
  and moving containers 159
  and mung bean sprouts 182–3
  and pallet planters 118–19
  and paperwhites 164–5
  and poinsettia 172–3
  and pot feet 158

217

and potting on 18–19
and storing containers 156–7
and watering 96
and winter colour 212–13
and winter protection 144, 160
see also soil blocks
copper rings 57
cordons 191
coreopsis 75
crab apple 189
cranefly larva 126–7
crocus 133, 142
cutting back 136–7
cuttings
　hydrangea 102–3
　lavender 100–1
　rose 114–15, 201, 204–5
　semi-ripe/semi-hardwood 102–3
　softwood 66
　in water 66–7
cyclamen 134, 135

D

daddy longlegs 126–7
daffodils 24, 132, 142
dahlia 56, 136
　cactus 53
　collarette 53
　decorative 53
　pompon 53
　starting tubers 52–3
　varieties 53
　winter protection 160–1
damsel bugs 39
deadheading 24, 68, 73, 80, 84–5
December 172–83
deciduous plants 206
delphinium 56, 107
dew 40, 41
dianthus 212–13
Dicksonia antarctica 87
digging 36–7, 82, 192
diseases 20, 117, 201
　see also fungal diseases
division 38
dormancy 82, 186, 188, 192, 200, 202, 207
drainage, lawns 45, 46–7

E

Eccremocarpus 85
echinacea 75, 136, 137
echinops 136
elder, common 189
eryngium 137
espaliers 191
evaporation 20, 21
evergreens 64–7, 135, 206

F

fat balls 178–9
February 142, 200–13
feeding plants 50, 116
　bulbs 24
　controlled-/slow-release feed 25, 92, 93, 116
　and DIY compost 88, 91
　and the Hampton hack 73
　hanging baskets 73, 92
　and heatwaves 96
　high-nitrogen feed 50, 92, 93
　lawns 49, 93
　liquid feed 92, 93
　pots 92
　quick-release feed 92, 93
　roses 25
fermentation 89
ferns 54–5
Festuca glauca 135
fir
　Fraser 175
　Nordmann 175
fish 167
flues 91
forks 12, 46–7
fountains 167
foxglove 136
fritillary 142
frogs 56, 166
frost 28, 53, 60, 86, 136, 137, 144, 155, 160–1, 166, 207, 211–12
　protection 158–9
fruit trees
　pruning 112–13, 190–1
　winter washing 180–1
fuchsia 161

fungal diseases 20, 69, 117, 132, 169
fungi 163, 180–1, 193

G

garden furniture 130–1
Geranium 67, 199
　G. endressii 106
　G. phaeum 106
　G. sylvaticum 106, 107
germination 20
getting started 10–21
gladiolus 161
graft unions 193
grass trimmers 42–3
grasses 54, 135, 136, 206
　see also lawns
gravel 168
greenfly 39, 180–1
greenhouses 143
grit 196
growth, directing 15

H

Hampton hack 106–7
hand shears 64
hanging baskets 72–3, 92, 134
hardening off 60, 211
hardy plants 55, 62, 87, 95, 166, 212
hawthorn 189
heat treatment 31
heather 134, 135
heatwaves 96
hedge trimmers 13, 64
hedgehogs 56
hedges 64–7, 82–3
helenium 75
helianthus 75
heliotrope 85
herbs 94–5
　see also specific herbs
heuchera 54–5
holiday watering 108–9
holly 64
honeysuckle 26–7, 70
hori hori knives 13, 30, 48
hornbeam 140
horse chestnut 140

horticultural fleece 60, 159
hoses 13, 121
   settings 20
   summer protection 97
   on wheels 97
   winter preparation 152–3
hosta 54–5, 56, 136
hoverflies 39
hyacinth 128–9, 132
Hydrangea 14, 136
   'Annabelle' 28
   climbing 80–1
   cuttings 67, 102–3
   H. macrophylla 29
   H. quercifolia 29
   new wood 28
   old wood 28, 29
   panicle 28
   pruning 28–9, 80–1
hylotelephium 75

I

insulation 144, 152, 154, 159–60
ivy 67, 70, 134, 135

J

January 184–99
Japanese maple 189
   see also acer
July 96–107
June 78–95

K

kale 195
kniphofia 86, 87

L

lacewings 39
ladybirds 39, 146
laurel 64
lavender 14, 61, 100–1, 110–11
lawn mowers 13
lawns
   aerating 45, 46–7
   and ants 99
   clover 50–1
   feeding 49, 93
   and grass trimmers 42–3
   last mow of the year 155
   and leatherjackets 126–7
   levelling 124–5
   and moss 44, 45
   mowing 40–1, 44, 124, 155
   overseeding 48–9
   patch repair 49
   planting bulbs in 142
   scarification 44–5
   slow growth 41
   top-dressings 45, 49
   and weeds 48, 49
leaf mould 140, 168, 196
leatherjackets 126–7
leylandii 64
lifting plants 160
lilac 85
lily, canna 86–7, 144, 160–1
loam 16, 17
lobelia 199
log stores 141
loppers 64
lupins 107

M

magnolia 188
March 24–39, 142
May 60–75
mealworms 178–9
methyl bromide (MB) 118
microclimates 159
microgreens 194–5
mildew 117
mint 67, 107
Miscanthus sinensis 135
misting plants 21
monarda 75, 107
mosquitos 121
moss 44, 45, 129
moving plants 36–7, 160
Musa basjoo 87
mulching 69, 140, 144
   guide 168–9
   and heatwaves 96
   and hedges 83
   and winter protection 161
   wood mulch 184
mung bean sprouts 182–3
mycorrhizal fungi 193

N

narcissus paperwhites 164–5
nematodes 57, 126–7
nepeta 74–5, 75
newts 56, 166
nigella 136
nitrogen fixation 50
November 150–69

O

oak 140
October 136–49
olive trees 62–3
organic matter 17

P

pak choi 195
pallets
   pallet bug hotels 146–7
   pallet planters 118–19
palms, phoenix 86, 87
pansy 85, 135, 212–13
paperwhites 164–5
parsley 95
paths, weed-free 32–3
patios 32–3, 58–9, 99
pear 112–13, 190
pelargonium 85, 199
penstemon 75, 161
perennials
   division 38
   and the Hampton hack 106–7
   mulching 168
   and winter interest 136
   see also specific perennials
pesticides 98
   homemade 39
pests 39, 56–7, 60, 91, 126–7, 133, 180–1
petunia 85
phlox 75
phoenix palm 86, 87

pieris 140
pinching out 211
pine needles 140
planters, pallet 118–19
poinsettia 172–3
polyanthus 85
ponds, winter care 166–7
poppy 107, 136
potting on 18–19
predators, natural 56, 127
pressure-washing 58–9
primula 212–13
privet 64
   propagation
      division 38
      roses 204–5
      in water 66–7
      see also cuttings; seed(s)
propagators 198–9
   protecting plants
      from pests 56–7, 133
   for winter 144–5, 160–1, 184, 207
pruning 14–15, 166
   citrus trees 207
   climbing hydrangea 80–1
   climbing roses 202–3
   evergreen hedges 64–7
   fruit trees 112–13, 190–1
   grasses 206
   honeysuckle 26–7
   hydrangea 28–9, 80–1
   lavender 61, 110–11
   olive trees 62–3
   ornamental trees 188–9
   roses 69, 200–4
   wisteria 78–9, 186–7
pulmonaria 54–5

R

radish 195
rakes 44, 49
   levelling 125
red hot pokers 86, 87
rhizomes 160
rhododendron 85, 140
rosemary 67, 95

roses
   bare-root 193
   black spot 69
   climbing 200, 202–3
   cuttings 114–15, 201, 204–5
   deadheading 68, 85
   feeding 25
   floribunda 200
   hybrid tea 200
   mulching 168
   patio 200
   propagation 204–5
   pruning 69, 200–4
   rambling 202–3
   shrub 200
   types of 200
rudbeckia 75, 136, 137
runners, strawberry 34–5, 104–5
rust 162–3

S

sage 95
salt 32–3
Salvia 106, 161, 199
   S. 'Blauhügel' 106
   S. 'Mainacht' 106, 107
sand 47, 124–5
sandy soil 16–17
scarification 44–5
secateurs 12, 14–15, 24, 26, 64, 69, 84
   cleaning 162–3
second flushes 106–7
sedum 75, 136
seed heads 136, 138
seed pods, wisteria 78–9
seed(s)
   clover 51
   collection 137
   microgreens 194–5
   overseeding lawns 48–9
   self-seeding 136
   storage 138–9
   summer bedding 198–9
   sweet pea 210–11
self-seeding 136
September 124–35
shade 54–5, 96
shears 64

shredders 184
shrubs 85, 168, 169
silica gel 139
silt 17
slow worms 56
slugs and snails 56–7, 60
snap dragon 199
snowdrop 133
soap and water 39
soil
   compaction 41, 46–7
   preparation 86
   testing 16–17
   texture triangles 17
soil blocks 196–7
spades, border 12
sphagnum moss 129
spiders 146
spring 22–75
sprouts, mung bean 182–3
spruce
   blue 175
   Norway 175
spurs 113
staking plants 83
standard trees 191
Stipa tenuissima 135
strawberry 34–5, 104–5
summer 76–121
sunlight 33, 97
sunny conditions 21
sustainability 175
sweet chestnut 140
sweet pea 185, 199, 210–11
sycamore 140

T

taps, insulation 152, 154
tender plants 52–3, 86–7, 166
terracotta 158–9
thatch, removal 44–5
thyme 95
toads 56
tomato feed 24, 92
tools 12–15, 30–1, 162–3
top-dressing 45, 49
topsoil 48, 51, 83, 124–5, 196
transpiration 21
tree fern 86, 87, 144

tree peony 85
trees 168, 169
    pruning citrus 207
    pruning fruit 190–1
    pruning ornamental 188–9
    winter washing 180–1
    see also specific trees
trellises 185, 186
tropical gardens 86–7, 144–5, 172–3
troubleshooting
    ants 98–9
    compost 91
    heatwaves 96
    and homemade pesticide 39
    protecting containers from frost 158–9
    protecting garden hoses 97, 152–3
    and protecting tropical plants 144–5
    slugs and snails 56–7
    weeds 30–1
trowels, hand 12
tubers 160
tulip 24, 132, 150
tulip fire 132
twine 13

V

vases, bulb 129
vermiculite 196
veronica 107
veronicastrum 75
vinegar 32–3
viola 72, 135, 212–13
Virginia creeper 70

W

walnut 140
wasps, parasitic 39
water butts 120–1
water features 121, 166–7
waterfalls 167
watering 20–1, 25, 69
    and ants 99
    before a frost 158
    Christmas trees 177
    hanging baskets 73
    heatwaves 96
    holiday 108–9
    and moving plants 36
    myths 21
watering systems, automatic 108
weed pullers 31
weeding 30–1, 168
    lawns 48, 49
    perennials weeds 48
weedkiller
    chemical 30
    homemade 32–3
Wildlife & Countryside Act 1981 64
willow 67
winter 170–213
    preparation for 143–5, 152–5, 158–63, 166–7
winter aconite 133
winter interest 136
winter protection 144–5, 160–1, 184, 207
winter washing 180–1
wire-brush cleaners 31
wisteria 70, 78–9, 186–7
wooden furniture 130
wool 56
woolly aphid 180–1
wormeries 88–9

Y

yew 64

ACKNOWLEDGEMENTS

AUTHOR ACKNOWLEDGEMENTS

First and foremost, thank you to everyone who has followed, liked, commented, or shared my content over the past few years. Without you, this book simply wouldn't exist. Every message, photo, and question you've sent has kept me inspired and reminded me why I started sharing my garden in the first place.

To my wife, thank you for your endless support and patience, for letting the garden (and the filming equipment) slowly take over our lives, and for giving me the space to chase an idea that turned into a full-blown career.

To my daughter, you make me want to be better every single day. You remind me to look closely, ask questions, and find joy in the small things growing quietly around us.

To my parents, thank you for giving me muddy boots, pocketfuls of conkers, and a lifelong love of the outdoors. You planted the first seed, quite literally.

And finally, to everyone who's ever picked up a trowel because of something I shared, thank you. This book is for you. Keep growing, keep experimenting, and never stop finding magic in the soil.

PUBLISHER ACKNOWLEDGEMENTS

DK would like to thank Manpreet Kaur for the picture research, Katie Hewett for the proofread, Lisa Footitt for the index, and Adam Brackenbury for the repro work.

PICTURE CREDITS

The publisher would like to thank the following for their kind permission to reproduce their photographs:

(Key: a-above; b-below/bottom; c-centre; f-far; l-left; r-right; t-top)

Alamy Stock Photo: David Burton 211r, Tim Gainey 189tl, 189tc, GCFitzpatrick Photos 88br, imageBROKER.com GmbH & Co. KG / Arco / O. Diez 189bc, Alex Ramsay 189br, Chris Rout 189bl, Leonid Shtandel 175cb, Graham Turner 126cr, Deborah Vernon 140; **Dreamstime.com:** Maria Abrashkina 75cb (Phlox), Anastasiia Akh 42br, Alexki23 95tl, Andersastphoto 107ca, Aleksandra Averina 213br, Anthony Baggett 87tl, 107tl, Tatiana Belova 75tc, Betricesara 75ca, Alexandr Blinov 135tl, Vladimir Blinov 213tl, Irina Borsuchenko 107cra, Tom Brandt 161bc, 213tr, Denys Braslavets 175tl, Catarii 55bl, Norman Chan 161br, Amphawan Chanunpha 213c, Colloidial 75c, Perry Correll 55br, Cshirk2 107br, Danako 107tr, Dawnmercer 75tr, Debu55y 75cra (Helenium), 213bl, Natalia Dobrovolska 135ca, Elenarostunova 107bc, Elfthryth 95br, Eugenesergeev 161ca, Faithiecannoise 87br, Randy Fletcher 85tl, Fotofix 94bl, Elizaveta Galitskaya 199bc, Gardendreamer 95tr, GeorgianBayBoudoir 88bc, Gkoultouridis 129bl, Nicola Gordon 55tc, Gratysanna 107tc, Patryk Gruszka 137r, Lijuan Guo 75crb (Rudbeckia), Gabor Havasi 67tr, Honza1 55tr, Imladris 67crb, 199c, Irishka777 67bc, James53145 107bl, Jennyrainbow 199cr, Sirle Kabanen 28br, Katinka2014 167tl, Kclarksphotography 75cra, Kewuwu 172, Andrey Kozlov 107clb, Oksana Krasiuk 135bc, Paulina Kurpiewska 53cra, Kurylo54 135clb, Leklek73 53cr, 75cb, 85bl, 212, Ihar Mamchyts 55tl, 161cra, Markstahl 67tc, Mayerberg 107cla, Katarzyna Mazurowska 75cb, Tom Meaker 85bc, 161cr, Milladilla 199br, Minaret2010 81r, Nivi 199cra, Oseland 107crb, Palabra 135cla, Michal Paulus 75br, Natalia Pavlova 67cb, William Perry 53crb, Gaid Phitthayakormsilp 135bl, Agata Pietrzak 75cr, Prambuwesas 53br, Jon Rehg 161tl, Tina Rencelj 67c, Paveerisa Sarutwattananont 29bl, Sjankauskas 135cb, Lenka Šoolíková 85tc, Starast 67br, Liz Van Steenburgh 189tr, Stef22 107cb, Andreea Stefan 95bl, Steve5181 75crb, 161c, Viroj Suttisima 85tr, Svetlanais 135tc, Terezie 75ca (Echinacea), Kheng Ho Toh 88c, Ukrphoto 85br, Lori Walter 55bc, Westhimal 199ca, Dusan Zidar 67cr; **Jason Ingram:** 4, 6, 8-9, 13cr, 40, 43r, 44-45, 46cr, 47, 48bl, 50, 57br, 70, 72-73, 90-91, 93, 96-97, 99l, 147r, 152-153, 154, 158-159, 166, 167cr, 167bc, 198, 199l, 206-207, 214-215, 224.

Editorial Director Ruth O'Rourke
Project Editor Lucy Philpott
Gardening Design Manager Barbara Zuniga
Design Assistant Noor Ali
Senior Production Editor Tony Phipps
Senior Production Controller Stephanie McConnell
Jacket and Sales Material Coordinator Serena Sclocco
Art Director Maxine Pedliham
Publishing Director Stephanie Jackson

Editorial Nicola Hodgson
Design Sarah Snelling
Cover illustration Eleanor Ridsdale

First published in Great Britain in 2026 by
Dorling Kindersley Limited
20 Vauxhall Bridge Road,
London SW1V 2SA

The authorised representative in the EEA is
Dorling Kindersley Verlag GmbH. Arnulfstr. 124,
80636 Munich, Germany

Text copyright © Michael Griffiths 2026
Michael Griffiths has asserted his right to be identified as
the author of this work
Copyright © 2026 Dorling Kindersley Limited
A Penguin Random House Company
10 9 8 7 6 5 4 3 2 1
001–357170–Apr/2026

All rights reserved.
No part of this publication may be reproduced, stored in or introduced into a retrieval system, or transmitted, in any form, or by any means (electronic, mechanical, photocopying, recording, or otherwise), without the prior written permission of the copyright owner. DK values and supports copyright. Thank you for respecting intellectual property laws by not reproducing, scanning or distributing any part of this publication by any means without permission. By purchasing an authorised edition, you are supporting writers and artists and enabling DK to continue to publish books that inform and inspire readers. No part of this publication may be used or reproduced in any manner for the purpose of training artificial intelligence technologies or systems. In accordance with Article 4(3) of the DSM Directive 2019/790, DK expressly reserves this work from the text and data mining exception.

A CIP catalogue record for this book
is available from the British Library.
ISBN: 978-0-2417-9694-8

Printed and bound in China

www.dk.com

ABOUT THE AUTHOR

Since May 2023, Michael has been making gardening feel simple, engaging, and accessible for his audiences on Instagram, TikTok, YouTube, and Facebook. He started his journey on TikTok, where he created short videos documenting his own garden renovation, as a way of archiving all the work he had done. A follower asked for advice on underplanting olive trees and he decided to make a quick video explaining what he knew. The video took off and he discovered that there were a lot of people looking for help with their gardens. His now-signature "how-to" videos break gardening tasks down into quick, clear, no-nonsense advice that actually helps. It's his mission to provide accessible gardening instructions that don't make you feel like you need a degree in horticulture to get started. Most of his content is filmed in his own back garden in Bristol UK, where he lives with his wife, daughter, and Border Terrier.

@themichaelgriffiths
@themichaelgriffiths
@TheMichaelGriffiths
@TheMichaelGriffiths